STATE OF THE UNION

By Thomas Blood and Bruce Henderson

STATE OF THE UNION

A Report
On
President
Clinton's
First Four
Years
In Office

By Thomas Blood
and Bruce Henderson

Publisher: W. Quay Hays
Art Director: Chitra Sekhar
Managing Editor: Stephen Motika
Copy Editor: Steve Baeck

The Publisher wishes to thank a very special catalyst for this book. Eight-year-old Paris Hays, who is as insightful as he is inquisitive, came up with the idea for *State of the Union* after a short visit to the nation's capital. It is the Publisher's hope that this book will serve as a constructive means by which Paris and the millions of other American children across the nation can one day fairly and honestly judge their President and, in the process, continue to believe that people can make a positive difference.

For information:
General Publishing Group, Inc.,
2701 Ocean Park Blvd., Ste. 140, Santa Monica, CA 90405

Library of Congress Cataloging-in-Publication Data

Blood, Thomas.
    State of the Union: a report on President Clinton's first four
years in office/by Thomas Blood and Bruce Henderson.
                p.   cm.
    Includes index.
    ISBN 1-57544-008-3
    1. United States—Politics and government—1993- 2. Clinton,
Bill, 1946-   .   I. Henderson, Bruce B., 1946-   .   II. Title.
E885.B57 1996
973.929—dc20   96-29167
                                                                                    CIP

Printed in the USA by RR Donnelley & Sons Company
10 9 8 7 6 5 4 3 2 1

General Publishing Group
Los Angeles

Table of Contents

Bill Clinton's birthplace—Hope, Arkansas.

Prologue

He was the first President of the United States to be born after World War II. He grew up in a small town in a poor state. He was the first member of his family to go to college. When he was a boy, he lived for a while on a farm without an indoor toilet. It makes a good story—"not as good as being born in a log cabin," he has admitted, "but it's true."

He came from Arkansas, born one August day in 1946 at a place called Hope, population 1,000. He never knew his real father. His stepfather did not have a high school diploma and his grandfather, who was a true inspiration to him, had a sixth-grade education and ran a grocery store across the street from the cemetery. A fifth-generation Arkansan, the boy grew up in a segregated society but in a pro–civil rights family, one that endured alcohol abuse (his stepfather), domestic violence (his mother was beaten), and, later, drug addiction (his brother). In fact, at age 14, he was forced to stand up to his stepfather to stop the abuse once and for all.

He lived in a family where everybody worked long and hard—his mother and grandmother had full-time jobs to help make ends meet—and the kids were expected to study just as hard. But he also had a lot of opportunity given to him by his community, when others recognized his thirst for learning and his commitment to work hard and get ahead. He had attentive teachers at the public schools he attended. And when he needed scholarships and after-school jobs, he found them. Along the way, he saw what happened to good people who had no opportunity because they happened to be black, or because they happened to be poor, white, and isolated in the hills and hollows of the mountains of his home state.

As a 16-year-old, he made a fateful trip to Washington, D.C., with other delegates to the American Legion Boys Nation. On a sun-drenched White House lawn, he met his and his generation's idol: President John F. Kennedy. Over six feet tall, even then, the impressionable, beaming boy looked eye-to-eye with the popular leader of the western world as he returned his handshake and began thinking about a career in politics.

He would return to the nation's capital several years later to attend Georgetown University, where he earned a bachelor's degree. Then, on to Yale Law School, and, finally, a journey across the Atlantic to Oxford as a Rhodes scholar. When his schooling was completed, he returned home and joined the law school faculty at the University of Arkansas. He began his public service a few years later, when he was elected state attorney general, and, soon after, the country's youngest governor.

His name, of course: William Jefferson Clinton.

These past four years the world has come to know a lot about the boy from Hope who became a world leader. He himself has talked much about his life, his family, and his vision for our country. What he had learned about responsibility and opportunity while growing up would, for him, all meld into an idea of what America is about; one that he promised to work toward.

"We never thought there was a mountain we couldn't climb, a river we couldn't ford, or a problem we couldn't solve," he told the nation, because that's what he believes. Here was a leader right out of a Horatio Alger story.

But being President of the U.S.A. is the big time—probably the highest mountain there is to climb. Even with his considerable experience in executive government, the young President was surprised at how quickly the honeymoon ended once he entered the White House and began his job as Chief Executive. His adversaries tirelessly attempted to paint a picture of a President hobbled by character flaws. The media routinely pointed out his public wavering on issues, provoking questions about just what Bill Clinton stood for. He has endured personal tragedies, sensational innuendo, political setbacks, and public triumphs in the glare of the national spotlight. As a result, he has ridden a roller coaster of public approval for his performance in his first four years.

But now, at the end of the first term of the 42nd President of the United States, it is time to tune out the rhetoric, push aside the distractions, and focus on what's important. The real concern for Americans, especially on the eve of a Presidential election, is this: What can we expect from our President? What kind of President has Bill Clinton been these last four years? Has he kept his promises to us? When he has taken action, was he effective? What exactly has he accomplished?

These are the questions to which all Americans deserve answers.

Authors' Note

Most Americans may be unaware of the basic responsibilities of the President of the United States as described in the U.S. Constitution—duties that must be performed even if he or she does nothing else. This may be because there has never been a universal standard by which citizens can go down a checklist to judge a President's performance.

Coauthor Tom Blood came up with a simple solution for providing a tool by which to "grade" a President's performance. It is rooted in something very familiar to virtually everyone: a school report card, using as its "subjects" the duties of the President as clearly defined by Article Two of the U.S. Constitution. In establishing the three distinct sections of a report card, we were able to produce a yardstick by which to measure a presidency:

Core Curriculum - Just as in high school or college, core curriculum represents the bare minimum we can expect from a President—the reading, writing, and arithmetic of a presidency.

Electives - Every student can elect to take on more than the core curriculum—in the case of a President this translates into campaign promises.

Extra Credit - Just as in the classroom, there are certain intangible factors that are worthy of merit. For the President, this includes commitment, leadership, and planning for the future.

We have not endeavored to give grades for President Bill Clinton's first term in office. Instead, we have revisited his campaign promises, speeches, legislative record and executive actions to provide the facts about what he and his Administration have accomplished so that readers will have all the information they need to grade the performance of their President.

A wide range of sources was used, including Internet and library research conducted by Stephen Motika of General Publishing Group and Theresa Sanders of Therra Technologies. On-line information data bases such as Dow Jones, the New York Times, the Washington Post, the Congressional Record, Census Bureau, Grolier, and Info Track were utilized, thereby giving us access to an extensive collection of newspapers and periodicals. Television news transcripts were provided by Burrelle's Information Services and Journal Graphics. Other persons who merit special thanks: Dawn Alexander, Robert Budway, Tom Burgess, Whitney Casey, J.B. Dilzheimer, Chris Duda, Scott Freda, Rich Gold, Glen Hicks, Rob Houseman, Caleb King, Ken Markowitz, Garth Neuffer, Steve Powell, Ann Rowan, Richard Sullivan, Kris Van Geisen and Jimmy Walter. Information was also obtained from the Democratic National Committee and Republican National Committee, both in Washington, D.C.

Acknowledgments

I'd like to thank my manager and friend Peter Miller of PMA Literary and Film Management, my beautiful wife Debbie and our children Sean and Kelli for their never-ending love and support, as well as my Dad and Mom and the rest of my family.
—*Tom Blood*

In agentry and friendship, Mike Hamilburg.
—*Bruce Henderson*

PART ONE

CORE CURRICULUM

In the nation's schools at practically every level, "core curriculum" represents the very basics. Similarly, core curriculum herein represents the "reading, writing, and arithmetic" of the presidency, based on passages in the United States Constitution. Virtually every provision of this venerable guideline to democracy has been interpreted over the years in many different ways. For over 200 years, its various clauses, provisions, and amendments have been touchstones of debate for Americans on a wide range of social issues— from gun control to V chips, school prayer to the Internet. This book's use of the Constitution is yet another means by which to consider its wisdom.

The Preamble reads:

"We, the people of the United States, in order to form a more perfect Union, establish justice, insure domestic tranquility, provide for the common defense, promote the general welfare, and secure the blessings of liberty to ourselves and our posterity, do ordain and establish this Constitution for the United States of America."

Article Two, which defines the power of the executive branch and grants the President the authority to serve as Commander-in-Chief, requires the President to take the following oath before assuming office: "I do solemnly swear that I will faithfully execute the office of the President of the United States, and will, to the best of my ability, preserve, protect, and defend the Constitution of the United States."

These fundamental powers and responsibilities, coupled with the sworn oath of the President to defend the Constitution, can reasonably be held to represent the minimal functions Americans can expect from their President. At a minimum, they are:

1. Establish Justice
2. Insure Domestic Tranquility
3. Provide for the Common Defense
4. Promote the General Welfare
5. Secure the Blessings of Liberty to Ourselves
    and Our Posterity
6. Serve as Commander-in-Chief

When all is said and done, these are the basic duties to be fulfilled by the President of the United States.

President's Duty: Establish Justice

Overseeing justice is a vital responsibility for any U.S. President. This duty includes addressing crime and its prevention, helping to safeguard the rights of law-abiding citizens, and making appointments to the federal bench to ensure that a climate of fairness and equality exists in federal courts.

Crime

Brady Bill

The Brady Handgun Violence Prevention Act
PL 103 - 159
Sponsor: Rep. Charles E. Shumer (D-New York)

The insistent refrain of the National Rifle Association (NRA), one of the most powerful lobbying forces on Capitol Hill is "Guns don't kill people—people kill people." This is but one side of a passionate national debate raging over whether or not so many Americans would be killed by guns every year if guns were more difficult to purchase.

The NRA took great offense to the Brady Bill, attempting to block it by framing it as a Constitutional issue with protests that any type of handgun control would be a first step toward the government's eventual abridgment of the citizenry's right to bear arms. By the time President Clinton entered the White House, the bill had long been blocked in Congress by strong opposition led by the Republican Party and the NRA.

President Clinton announces his signing of the Brady Bill as James Brady looks on.

Named after James Brady, the former White House press secretary shot in the head and permanently paralyzed in the 1981 assassination attempt on President Ronald Reagan, and spearheaded by his determined wife Sarah Brady, the bill proposed a five-day waiting period on all handgun sales in the United States. The wait would not only serve as a "cooling off" period for a new gun owner in the event there was a sinister reason for the purchase, but, most importantly, would require all would-be handgun purchasers to submit to a criminal background check. The legislation called for $200 million a year to computerize criminal background information so an instant-check system could be created within the next five years.

Convinced that the Brady Bill could be an effective way to reduce gun-related crimes, President Clinton had publicly supported the legislation even before his election in 1992. That year's statistics on handgun deaths were persuasive: In countries with strong gun laws, the handgun death rates were low: Great Britain, 33 people killed; Sweden, 36; Switzerland, 97; Japan, 60; Australia, 13; and Canada, 128. That same year in the United States, 13,220 people were killed by handguns. When handguns were added to all other types of firearms, the total number of people killed by guns in the U.S. in 1993 was 39,595.

The Clinton Administration and other handgun control advocates finally overcame the NRA's well-organized opposition to the Brady Bill, and it passed Congress in December 1993.

"How sweet it is, how long it took," said Jim Brady, his speech still impaired from his injury. "One day twelve years ago my life was changed forever by a disturbed young man with a gun. Until that time, I hadn't thought much about gun control. Maybe if I had, I wouldn't be stuck with these damned wheels."

In February 1995, the Bureau of Alcohol, Tobacco and Firearms (BATF) released its "Brady Law First Anniversary Survey." The survey canvassed 30 jurisdictions across America, and revealed that since the bill's passage, 3.5 percent of those individuals applying for gun purchases had applications denied. Among those stopped from obtaining handguns: 4,365 convicted felons, 945 fugitives, 649 illegal drug users, 97 persons under indictment, and 63 persons under temporary restraining orders for alleged stalking. Based on this limited sampling and using conservative assumptions, the BATF projected that nationwide the Brady Law had stopped approximately 70,000 convicted felons, drug offenders, fugitives, and other prohibited purchasers from making over-the-counter purchases of handguns. After the second anniversary of the Brady Law, a similar survey of 22 law enforcement agencies in 15 states found that in these jurisdictions alone, nearly 15,000 felons and other prohibited purchasers were prevented from buying handguns in 1995.

Crime Bill
Violent Crime Control and Law Enforcement Act of 1994
PL 103 - 322
Sponsor: Rep. Jack Brooks (D-Texas)

According to the National Crime Victimization Survey, in 1994, U.S. residents age 12 or older were affected by approximately 42.4 million crimes—10.9 million were violent in nature. For every 1,000 persons age 12 or older, there occurred two rapes, three assaults with serious injury, and four robberies.

At a time when crime was noted by public opinion polls to be the greatest concern of Americans, President Clinton introduced and saw Congress approve his Crime Bill of 1994, considered by many to be the most comprehensive anticrime measure in U.S. history. It has been endorsed by a majority of the nation's leading law enforcement groups, including the National Sheriffs' Association, National Association of Police Organizations, Federal Law Enforcement Officers Association, National Black Police Association, Fraternal Order of Police, International Union of Police Associations, Major City Chiefs Association, and the National Troopers Coalition. In 1995, the nation's largest cities saw an overall decrease in crime of 6 percent, while nationwide the number of murders fell 8 percent, one of the largest decreases in more than 30 years.

The bill's features include:

• **100,000 New Police Officers.** A key provision provides funding for 100,000 new police officers nationwide. To date, more than 1,200

cities and towns have received grants to hire more police, resulting in nearly 60,000 new officers on the nation's streets.

- **Community Policing.** Funding was increased by $1.3 billion for community policing, a partnership between the police and the public working together in a joint effort to prevent crime and promote safety. Catching on in cities large and small around the country, community policing not only increases police visibility in the streets, but also gives residents a voice in setting police priorities and a contributing role in keeping the peace in their neighborhoods.

- **Three Strikes and You're Out.** This federal provision requires mandatory life in prison for career violent offenders convicted of federal crimes such as bank robbery and smuggling. Three-strikes laws are on the books in more than a dozen states, pushed forth by an electorate fed up with crime. Clearly, the purpose of these laws was to ensure longer prison sentences and greater punishment for those who have been convicted of serious and violent felonies. In some states, however, the reality is that there isn't enough room in existing prisons to house the new influx of repeat offenders. As most state three-strikes laws are not tied to building new prison facilities, local authorities have sometimes been forced to release other inmates early to make room for those convicted under three-strikes laws.

- **Federal Prison Construction.** Additional funding was earmarked for the construction of more federal prisons, needed to house the increased inmate population anticipated from the new three-strikes law.

- **Death Penalty Expansion.** The number of offenses punishable by the death penalty was expanded by nearly 60 additional categories of violent felons, including terrorists, drug kingpins, and murderers of federal law enforcement officers.

- **Creation of the National Police Corps.** The institution of the National Police Corps helps put military personnel and unemployed veterans to work in law enforcement.

- **Prevention and Rehabilitation.** More money is used to fund drug treatment programs for criminal addicts and boot camps for youthful offenders.

• **Violence Against Women Act.** As an integral part of his anti-crime legislative package, the President signed this act to provide new grants to bolster local law enforcement and prosecutors, and a multitude of victims' services. The Act tripled funding for battered women's shelters, improved police and court response to domestic violence crimes, added lighting in public places, and required sex offenders to pay restitution. To coordinate these various new programs, the act provided for the Justice Department to establish a Violence Against Women Office.

• **National Domestic Violence Hotline.** The Administration established this 24-hour hotline service (800-799-7233) to provide callers with immediate crisis information, counseling, and referrals. Operators offer information on domestic violence, emergency shelters, legal advocacy, assistance programs, and social services. The Hotline, which began operation in early 1996, has to date received more than 20,000 calls from victims of domestic violence, and their families and concerned friends.

The issue of domestic violence cannot be fully addressed, President Clinton stated in July 1996, until the nation's "completely overburdened" 911 emergency number system is fixed. The majority of callers to 911 misuse the system—calling for nonemergencies. At the same time, victims who need immediate police help often receive busy signals. The President has recommended that police departments work with local phone companies to come up with another easy-to-remember number for residents to contact police for nonemergency calls.

• **Assault Weapons Ban.** Perhaps the hardest-fought provision of President Clinton's first-term crime agenda was the Assault Weapons Ban. Like the Brady Bill, it was vehemently opposed by the NRA, which expressed concern for those Americans who enjoy hunting. Proponents of the ban claimed that assault weapons are designed and manufactured only to "hunt people."

The ban prohibits the sale, transfer, or importation of 19 military-style assault weapons, much like the rifles used in the recent massacres in Scotland and Australia in which the loss of life totaled 42 unsuspecting people, half of which were children under eight years of age. Banned weapons include the AK-47, Uzi submachine gun, revolving-

Vice President Al Gore gestures toward a table displaying some of the 19 types of assault weapons banned by the Administration's Crime Bill.

cylinder shotguns such as the "Street Sweeper" and "Striker 12," as well as the deadly TEC-9 assault pistol, capable of firing more than 50 times before reloading—the weapon of choice (two were used) in a 1993 attack on a San Francisco law office by a vengeful former client that left nine people dead. At the same time, the bill specifically protects more than 650 legitimate sporting weapons.

Every major law enforcement organization in the country supported passage of the ban against assault weapons, including the Fraternal Order of Police, the National Sheriffs' Association, and the International Association of Chiefs of Police.

After September 1994, the ban prevented domestic gun manufacturers from producing assault weapons and ammunition clips holding more than 10 rounds, and also excluded the importation of all types of assault weapons. While assault weapons and ammo clips holding more than 10 rounds produced prior to the date of the ban can still be sold, the price of these weapons has nearly tripled—in some instances to more than $2,000—making them less affordable.

Since its passage, the Assault Weapons Ban has resulted in an 18 percent decline in assault weapons crimes in 1995. Moreover, the number of assault weapons recovered by police officers has declined nearly 48.6 percent.

The CIA Shootings

In pushing for the assault weapons ban, President Clinton more than once referred to a tragic incident that took place only four days after he took office: five Central Intelligence Agency employees were randomly gunned down at the gate of CIA Headquarters in Langley, Virginia.

A Pakistani national, Mir Aimal Kansi, armed with a Chinese-made semiautomatic AK-47 assault rifle equipped with a 30-round clip—both since outlawed under the Assault Weapons Ban—opened fire on a line of cars waiting to enter the 258-acre CIA complex. With his gun barrel only inches away from the drivers' windows, he calmly walked up the line of cars firing in bursts, killing two civilian office workers and wounding three other employees. In the chaos that followed, the assailant returned to his car and drove away.

Kansi was identified when his roommate filed a missing person's report. The description matched the CIA shooter. In his apartment, police found the AK-47 used in the attack. By then, however, Kansi had slipped out of the country on a nonstop flight to his native country, where he disappeared into the terrorist underground. Law enforcement officials would eventually speculate that the gunman may have had a vendetta that went back to the CIA's weapons-supplying mission in the guerrilla war in Afghanistan, a neighbor of Pakistan.

In an effort to bring the person responsible for the killings to trial in the United States, federal agents followed the killer's trail halfway around the world. Thorny extradition issues further complicated the situation, creating contention between the highest levels of government in both countries. The Administration was forced to apply diplomatic pressure to assure cooperation from Pakistan.

Two years after the killings, Kansi finally entered a U.S. courtroom to face murder and other charges against him. At present, he is under guard at the U.S. Army Prison at Fort Leavenworth, Kansas, awaiting trial.

Cell Phones for Neighborhood Watch Groups

In about 20,000 locations across the country, neighborhood watch volunteers keep an eye on their streets and report problems to local police or fire departments. When they spot trouble, however, they are not always near a phone, causing authorities to receive delayed reports.

In an attempt to arm citizen watch groups with the same high-tech tools as the street gangs and drug dealers, President Clinton announced in July 1996 that his Administration had persuaded the cellular phone industry to donate 50,000 phones to help neighborhoods fight crime. The donated cell phones will be preprogrammed to local law enforcement and other emergency numbers. The idea is that any citizen patrollers who encounter an emergency or some other suspicious circumstance could call for help immediately.

The Cellular Telecommunications Industry Association, a trade group of wireless carriers, will provide phones and free airtime to groups certified by the Community Policing Consortium (CPC). The consortium includes several police groups and the Justice Department's community policing department. Neighborhood groups seeking phones should contact their local police, or they can reach the CPC at 1-800-833-3085.

Iraqi Plot to Assassinate Former President George Bush

During and after the Persian Gulf War, Saddam Hussein, through his controlled media, had threatened that President George Bush would be held personally responsible for the war and would be hunted down and punished, even after he left office. Shortly after his defeat in the 1992 election, the former President accepted an invitation from the grateful government of Kuwait to visit their country.

Then, in February 1993, sixteen suspects—including two Iraqi nationals—were arrested by Kuwaiti authorities in a plot to assassinate former President Bush when he visited Kuwait City. Following the arrests, President Clinton ordered U.S. intelligence and law enforcement agencies to conduct a thorough and independent investigation. Based on that probe, compelling evidence was uncovered that the plot, involving a powerful remote-control car bomb made in Iraq, had been directed and pursued by the Iraqi Intelligence Service.

"This plot against a former President of the United States because of actions he took as President was an attack against our country and against all Americans," President Clinton said. A firm response was needed "to protect our sovereignty, to send a message to those who engage in state-sponsored terrorism, and to deter further violence against our people."

The President ordered U.S. forces, in April 1993, to launch a cruise missile attack on the Iraqi Intelligence Service's principal command and control facility in Baghdad. In all, 23 Tomahawk cruise missiles, launched from a U.S. cruiser in the Persian Gulf and a U.S. destroyer in the Red Sea, skimmed above the landscape from 50 to 300 feet at speeds up to 550 mph. Efforts had been made to minimize the loss of life by striking in the middle of the night and only at a military target. When the missiles struck, the facility associated with Iraq's support of terrorism was destroyed.

Victims' Rights

After opposing every other new Constitutional Amendment

proposed during his presidency, President Clinton announced, in June 1996, his intention to support an amendment to give victims a larger role in proceedings against the people accused of harming them. Describing the Constitution as "sacred," the President explained that amending it is not something he takes lightly, but he believed it was necessary to do so on this issue, as the justice system too often "ignores the rights of victims while so studiously protecting the rights of the accused."

The Administration had reportedly been weighing the issue since a proposed Constitutional amendment was put forth by Senators Dianne Feinstein (D-California) and Jon Kyl (R-Arizona) in the spring of 1996. A slightly weaker version was also introduced in the House by Representative Henry Hyde (R-Illinois).

Without endorsing either legislative proposal, President Clinton said he intended to support an amendment that would ensure that victims will be told when court proceedings and parole hearings will occur; give victims the right to attend all hearings; give victims the opportunity to make a statement about bail, sentencing, accepting a plea, and parole; make sure victims are notified when a defendant or convict escapes; and ensure victims the right to receive restitution from the defendant.

Many of these ideas are similar to the proposed Kyl-Feinstein amendment, the major exception being that President Clinton does not favor the Senate measure's proposal to give victims a right to demand the speedy trial of a defendant accused of harming them. Federal prosecutors fear that such a provision could force them to go to trial before their case is ready.

In order to enact a Constitutional Amendment, it must first be passed by two-thirds majorities in each house of Congress—the House of Representatives and the Senate—and then be ratified by three-fourths of the states. Noting that the process could take years, the President directed Attorney General Janet Reno to adopt a nationwide system to alert victims about court proceedings and help assure they will be heard in court.

The Courts

Certainly one of the more lasting effects a President can have on the country is through his appointments to the federal bench—not only the Supreme Court, but the entire federal judiciary of approximately 800 judges. Since taking office, President Clinton has made 147 judicial appointments at the district and appellate levels. According to the American Bar Association (ABA), the President's appointments have the highest combined competence rating of any group since President Dwight Eisenhower. From a standpoint of diversity, this same group includes the largest numbers of minority and women appointments in history.

On March 19, 1993, Supreme Court Justice Byron White announced his intention to retire, graciously allowing the President a large amount of time to select a suitable replacement. According to White House officials, the very next day, the President was

President Clinton announces Supreme Court Justice appointees Stephen Breyer (above) and Ruth Bader Ginsburg (left).

provided a list in some detail and depth of over 40 people. This diverse list included private lawyers, judges, political figures, and academics. Over 3,000 opinions were read by over 75 lawyers who worked in the selection process, all serving on a pro bono basis. The President consulted

broadly both on a bipartisan basis and on and off the Judiciary Committee in order to avoid the mistakes the Administration had just endured during a very intense selection process for attorney general.

The list was narrowed to three candidates: Secretary of the Interior Bruce Babbitt and two judicial figures—Stephen Breyer and Ruth Bader Ginsburg. All three survived the vetting process and background checks.

In June 1993, President Clinton made the first Supreme Court nomination by a Democrat in a generation. Judge Ginsburg, appointed to the court of appeals by President Carter in 1980, had been viewed as a centrist in her legal philosophy and a consensus-builder on an often divided court. Prior to her tenure on the bench, she had been a constitutional law and procedures professor at Columbia University Law School for nine years. In her private law practice, she had a strong record as a litigator on behalf of women's rights, including having had a role in winning virtually every Supreme Court case in the 1970s that invalidated laws discriminating against women. She had presented oral argument in the Supreme Court six times, prevailing in five of those cases. On abortion rights, Judge Ginsburg had left no ambiguity about her support for a woman's right to choose.

She received the American Bar Association's top rating of "exceptionally well qualified," and the Senate Judiciary Committee's vote to forward to the full Senate her Supreme Court appointment was on a unanimous, bipartisan vote. The Senate quickly confirmed her nomination.

A year later, President Clinton made his second appointment to the Supreme Court: Stephen Breyer, Chief Judge of the United States Court of Appeals for the First Circuit. Prior to a decade on the bench, he had served as chief counsel of the Senate Committee on the Judiciary. While in private practice, he had been a member of the Federal Sentencing Commission.

Judge Breyer's appointment also received the ABA's highest rating, was unanimously approved by the Senate Judiciary Committee, and was swiftly confirmed by the Senate. Court watchers agree that these two appointments have moved the court toward the center, providing a balance against the more conservative jurists who joined the court during previous Republican administrations.

President's Duty: Insure Domestic Tranquility

Perhaps more than most other places around the world, Americans experience a quality of life virtually devoid of civil strife and domestic unrest. But sudden, violent confrontations and tragic natural disasters do hit close to home with increasing frequency. Fortunately, this is a much more rare occurrence than in the days of the framers of the Constitution, who lived in a land still bearing the scars of bloody battles fought in order to secure independence. When they took up their collective pen and charged the President with insuring domestic tranquility, it was a vitally important task.

Now, two centuries later, insuring public safety and domestic tranquility still remains a fundamental duty that Americans expect of every occupant of the Oval Office. Over the past four years, Americans in widely diverse parts of the country—from our biggest cities to the quiet heartlands—have had their peace of mind shattered and physical safety threatened in an astonishing variety of ways—from violent crimes to bomb blasts, from fires to earthquakes, from floods to armed standoffs.

Public Safety

In the early 1990s, Gallup and other major public opinion polls indicated that a majority of Americans considered the rising crime rate to be a primary concern in their daily lives. In the wake of the Administration's 1994 Crime Bill, figures collected by the U.S. Bureau of Justice Statistics indicate that more than 90 percent of Americans are safer today, because of the declining crime rate, than they have been in two decades. The

alarming exception to this trend is America's teenagers, especially minorities, whose violent-death rate has been on the rise for several years.

Leading law enforcement agencies agree that "community policing," which is being emphasized in cities across the land, is beginning to have an effect on crime. They agree that other things may be working, too, such as hiring more officers, increasing uniform visibility on the streets, and enforcing stiffer sentencing for violent repeat offenders.

The FBI reports that combined incident reports for the U.S. in several major crime categories were down significantly in 1995 from the previous year. They are as follows:

Murder - down 8 percent
Robbery - down 7 percent
Rape - down 6 percent
Assault - down 3 percent
Auto theft - down 6 percent
Burglary - down 5 percent

Every region of the country is benefiting from lower crime rates, according to the FBI. The biggest winners are cities of more than one million people; they averaged a one-year 6 percent decrease (1995) in all reported crime. Murders are down in New York City 25 percent; in St. Louis, down 18 percent; in Los Angeles, down 21 percent; in Seattle, down 32 percent.

National Registry of Sex Offenders

In a speech to the U.S. Conference of Mayors in the summer of 1996, President Clinton said that recent efforts to monitor and deter sex offenders haven't gone far enough and he endorsed a national registry to track sexual predators as they cross state lines.

Establishing a national registry would expand upon the state registries for sex offenders that were mandated by the Clinton Administration's 1994 Crime Bill. The White House instructed Attorney General Janet Reno to study and report back in 60 days on how such a national system could be devised. Bipartisan legislation requiring a national registry is presently pending in Congress.

Airport Security

On July 25, 1996, in response to the recent tragedy of TWA Flight 800, President Clinton ordered heightened security measures for the nation's airports. While cautioning Americans "not to jump to conclusions" about the still undetermined cause of the crash of TWA 800, the President outlined the new security regulations that would be mandated by the Federal Aviation Administration to better protect airliners and passengers from terrorist bombs.

• Baggage and cargo will be subject to greater scrutiny. Among other things, curbside luggage check-in for passengers on international flights was prohibited.

• Passengers may face more thorough questioning about their baggage and carry-on items before they board flights.

• For all international flights, the airplane cabin, cockpit, and cargo areas will be thoroughly searched before passengers, baggage, and cargo are loaded aboard.

The President also directed Vice President Al Gore to establish a commission to develop a plan within 45 days for deploying new high-technology inspection machines capable of detecting the most sophisticated explosive. The Gore Commission will also review aviation safety, security, and the pace of modernization of the air-traffic control system.

Terrorism

World Trade Center Bombing

Approximately one month after the new President was inaugurated, during the middle of the lunch hour on Friday, February 26, 1993, a powerful explosive device detonated in the parking garage beneath the World Trade Center in New York City. The blast punched a 100-foot crater through four floors of concrete, knocked out power, communications,

On February 26, 1993, a bomb exploded beneath the World Trade Center.

and security systems, and filled the 110-story twin towers with thick smoke. Six people were killed, and more than 1,000 others injured.

In a letter to the *New York Times*, an unknown Islamic fundamentalist group calling itself the "Liberation Army Fifth Battalion" claimed responsibility. The group attributed the attack to its anger over U.S. support for Israel. The letter threatened other acts of sabotage against American civilians and military and nuclear targets unless the U.S. severed all relations with Israel and stopped its involvement in "internal" Middle East affairs.

The Justice Department established a task force for which the apprehension of the culprits was the number-one priority. Administration foreign-policy strategists drafted contingency plans that could be used if the trail led to a terrorist group outside the country or a renegade nation. "If there is an international aspect to this," said a State

Department spokesman, "it will be followed. The message that we wish to send out to terrorists is that no matter how long it takes, we're coming after you and we're going to get you."

Within 48 hours, FBI agents found in the pancaked parking structure traces of nitrate, an ingredient in dynamite. They also unearthed clues as to the identity of the vehicle that had carried the bomb.

Two days later, a 25-year-old Palestinian illegal immigrant was arrested by the FBI as he tried to reclaim the rental deposit on the van wrecked in the blast. Later that same day, his associate was also arrested. The next day, FBI agents seized chemicals and bomb parts in a New Jersey warehouse.

Over the next three weeks, five suspects were apprehended, including an Egyptian said to have been an organizer of the bombing. It was verified that one of the suspects had written the letter sent to the *New York Times.* A solid case was methodically built by federal agents and prosecutors. All five suspects were subsequently tried and convicted, and are presently serving life sentences in federal prisons.

Declaring the World Trade Center bombing a major disaster, President Clinton provided federal funds to pay for a sizable portion (75 percent) of the cost of emergency protective measures incurred by the state and local government—fire, police, ambulance, and other emergency services that responded to the disaster. The repair to the building itself was covered by private insurance—the final price tag was put at $600 million—and was not eligible for federal relief.

New York Governor Mario Cuomo issued a statement thanking President Clinton "on behalf of all New Yorkers" for the help. "This assistance," Cuomo said, "coupled with the superb performance of federal law enforcement agents, shows we can count on the federal government to be our partner in time of need."

Oklahoma City Bombing

Shortly after 8 A.M. on the morning of Wednesday, April 19, 1995, as Oklahomans were beginning their day, arriving at work and dropping their children at a day care center in the Alfred P. Murrah Federal

Building, the world itself seemed to erupt in a deafening roar accompanied by shock waves and blinding light.

In what would be the greatest loss from an episode of antigovernment domestic terror, 169 Americans—men, women, and innocent children, 19 of whom were infants—would be lost while simply carrying on with their daily lives in America's heartland.

At the time of the blast, President Clinton was sitting in the Oval Office with the Turkish prime minister. Both had been smiling for photographers when the White House press secretary came in, bent close to the President's ear, and quietly informed him that an explosion had destroyed part of a federal building in Oklahoma City.

After his official visitor departed, the President was told that heavy casualties were expected. When he confirmed that Attorney General Janet Reno had been called and that she'd already dispatched the FBI to the scene, the President turned on the television and had his first look at the terrible images of broken and bloodied children being pulled from the rubble. It made him "beyond angry," he later stated.

"Sometimes the real measure of a President's entire term comes down to his handling of a single crisis," *Time* magazine opined

The Alfred P. Murrah Building in downtown Oklahoma City was destroyed by a terrorist bomb on April 19, 1995.

One year after the tragedy, President Clinton honors the survivors and victims of the Oklahoma City bombing which claimed the lives of 169 people.

two weeks later in its ongoing coverage of the bombing. "At such moments, you're suddenly reminded that the presidency is an institution that people turn to in times of crisis and distress." In dealing with a tragedy such as the Oklahoma City bombing, a President must operate on two levels: systematically and symbolically.

Systematically, the President had Chief of Staff Leon Panetta promptly organize an interagency task force, which met in the "Situation Room" in the West Wing of the White House within an hour of the blast. The President told the group he planned to make a public statement, but before he did so, he needed to know as much as possible about what had happened. Briefed in person and over large videoconference screens by various agencies, task force members learned that authorities in Oklahoma City were working on, but had not yet developed firm leads in their efforts to apprehend the bombers. Meanwhile, it was determined by the task force that several provisions of federal law would allow for the death penalty to be sought against those responsible for the bombing.

Symbolically, when he went before the nation a few hours later, President Clinton spoke with a mixture of anger and sympathy. Calling the Oklahoma City bombers "evil cowards," he promised they would be tracked down, arrested, and "treated like killers." At memorial services for the victims, President Clinton mourned with all of Oklahoma City and much of the nation. In directing his remarks to the nation's children, he said: "What happened here was a bad thing, an evil thing. But we will bring to justice the people who did it. There is no place to hide."

Nine days after the bombing, Persian Gulf War veteran Timothy McVeigh was arrested, after being identified as the man who parked a rented truck carrying the bomb in front of the federal building. According to the FBI, McVeigh and his confederates, among them another Army vet named Terry Nichols, wrathful at the government over Waco, made and delivered the 4,800-pound bomb made from fuel oil and ammonium nitrate. They are both in custody awaiting trial.

Antiterrorism Bill
PL 104 - 132
Sponsor: Sen. Robert Dole (R-Kansas)

Shortly after the Oklahoma City bombing, the President challenged Congress to act swiftly in passing a strong bill that he could sign immediately to provide better tools and tougher penalties for the war against terrorism. House Speaker Newt Gingrich said Congress could act in 30 days to toughen antiterrorism laws. But House Republicans, led by key members of the conservative freshman class, slammed on the brakes.

A year later, there was still no antiterrorism bill. In his weekly radio address to the nation on April 13, 1996, President Clinton urged Congress to "Put the national interest before special interests," change course, and make good on its promise. He accused Congress of "foot-dragging" and bowing to such special interests as the National Rifle Association in blocking passage.

Twelve days later, 22 survivors of the Oklahoma City blast and 7 survivors of the 1993 World Trade Center bombing were with President Clinton as he signed into law the first antiterrorism measure of its kind, which authorized $1 billion in funding for federal law enforcement agencies to use in combating terrorism.

The new law expanded the government's power to exclude suspected foreign terrorists from the United States and established grant programs from funds raised, in part, by steep fines on convicted terrorists and others to help victims of terrorist attacks—a provision authored by Senator Patrick Leahy (D-Vermont), a former prosecutor. It also imposed unprecedented curbs on federal appeals by death-row inmates.

Despite the passage of the bill, the President admitted that it was not as tough as he wanted. For instance, Congress dropped a provision that would have made it easier to wiretap all phones used by suspected terrorists. "It was unfortunate Congress didn't approve authority for multi-point wiretaps," said assistant director of the FBI James Kallstrom, who in July 1996 would lead the investigation into the crash of TWA Flight 800. Kallstrom said the FBI desperately needed to enhance its ability to deal with new technologies—including E-mail, encrypted messages, and digital telephones—that terrorists and criminals are already using to communicate with each other. Congress also dropped from the antiterrorism bill a provision that would have required chemical markers in some explosive materials, making them easier to trace.

According to Anthony Lake, national security advisor to the White House, the tougher antiterrorism strategy has already paid off. Attempted terrorist attacks on New York City and American jumbo jets have been foiled. And the Clinton Administration has extradited and arrested more terrorists than all previous Administrations combined, Lake said.

Three days after the bombing at the Atlanta Olympics, President Clinton held a high-level White House summit with leaders of both parties to discuss better ways to deal with the threat of terrorism. He also renewed a call for Congress to adopt the wiretapping and high-tech "tagging" of explosives that it had cut out of the antiterrorism bill—liberals considered the measures an infringement on civil liberties, and conservatives believed they were too intrusive.

In the aftermath of the 1996 TWA Flight 800 crash and the Olympic bombing, public sentiment appears to have given these antiterrorism

measures new life. Representative Newt Gingrich (D-Georgia), pointing out that such tragedies "united all Americans," said Republicans may now be more open to considering additional antiterrorism legislation.

Militias and Cartels

The Siege of the Branch Davidian Compound in Waco, Texas

Two days after the World Trade Center bombing and 1,500 miles to the southeast, in the ruler-flat, tumbleweed countryside outside Waco, Texas, the U.S. government faced a far different kind of crisis.

The battle with religious cult leader David Koresh, who proclaimed

The siege at the Branch Davidian compound in Waco, Texas, ends as the grounds are engulfed in flames. Some 80 people perished.

himself the second coming of Jesus Christ, and his followers began when a team of agents from the Treasury Department's Bureau of Alcohol, Tobacco and Firearms (BATF) attempted to serve search warrants on the Branch Davidian compound. The BATF had developed reliable information that the sect had collected large amounts of weapons parts and munitions that could be used to manufacture illegal machine guns and grenades.

When the BATF agents arrived at the compound, search warrant in hand, they were ambushed by heavy automatic gunfire from numerous, well-fortified positions inside the compound. Later, there would be speculation that Koresh had been tipped off to the raid in a phone call from a local newspaper reporter, although it was never proven. Four agents died in the attack, and 20 others were injured, some seriously.

A siege ensued, and operational control at the scene shifted to the FBI. Fifty-one days later, on April 19, as much of the country watched on television, Koresh and most of his followers burned to death within their compound in a fiery blaze after FBI agents ordered Army tanks to punch holes in the walls so they could fire tear gas into the structure to end the standoff.

Only 9 of the 85 people inside escaped the inferno; 19 children died. Seventeen victims died of gunshot wounds, some believed to be self-inflicted. Coroners found victims, including children, shot by fellow Davidians, presumably to prevent them from escaping.

It was, in some respects, the first real crisis of the new Administration and it ended with controversy over the government's actions. President Clinton immediately ordered both the Treasury and Justice departments to conduct their own investigations of the incident. The Justice investigation would examine the FBI's role in the siege and the destructive fire that ended it, and Treasury would focus on the actions of the BATF.

Clearly, errors and miscalculations had been made by federal law enforcement. In examining the BATF's aborted attempt to serve the search warrant, for example, major gaps were discovered in planning, command, and control, as well as the gathering and analyzing of intelligence. Six BATF supervisors involved in the planning and execution of the raid were suspended.

The Justice Department report absolved the FBI of responsibility for the fiery ending to the standoff, finding that cult members had not only killed some of their own children but also set the blazes that consumed their compound. Also, a congressional investigation would find that the new attorney general, former Florida prosecutor Janet Reno, whose appointment had been confirmed only weeks prior to Waco, had carefully considered all appropriate options and had little other recourse in trying to end the long siege. In testifying before Congress, Reno had defended her decision to authorize use of tear gas to try to end the stalemate. The FBI faced an impossible situation that had gone on for nearly two months, she explained, and very much on her mind were the dangers for those who remained inside the compound—especially the children who reportedly were being sexually abused by Koresh.

After Waco, the Clinton Administration and Attorney General Reno were determined that different and more effective methods be found to handle such standoffs in the future. With input from the law enforcement community, Reno authorized new "use-of-force" guidelines for Justice and Treasury law enforcement agents. The policy spelled out the importance of using lesser force whenever feasible in dealing with suspects, and prohibited agents from using deadly force against any person "except as necessary" to protect themselves or another from "imminent" threat of death or serious injury.

Freemen Standoff

A group of determined, self-proclaimed "Freemen" holed up on a ranch in Montana in the spring of 1996. They included several offenders previously charged with writing bad checks and money orders and threatening a federal judge.

For nearly a year, local prosecutors and law enforcement officers had been unable to serve warrants on the armed Freemen, hunkered down in their self-proclaimed "Justus Township." When the Freemen made a videotape suggesting that they were planning some type of violent action in the area, the FBI stepped in.

A cattle guard on a dirt road had been upended and a thin wire stretched between two fence posts—a crude barricade thrown up by the Freemen. But it served its purpose to ward off and thereby hold at bay some 150 federal agents and assorted local police officers.

This was to be the first outing for the FBI's more cautious approach to crisis management. From the ashes of Waco had come this new way of heading off an armed clash and preventing loss of life. At Waco, investigations revealed that negotiators and tactical units were at times operating independently in an "uncoordinated and counterproductive fashion." As a result, the FBI had formed a new Critical Incident Response Group, composed of crisis negotiators, behavioral scientists, high-tech specialists, and a hostage rescue team. Group members were trained to value patience over reaction.

It took 81 days and a lot of talking to get the Freemen to surrender, but when the 26 antigovernment zealots walked out on their own accord, not a single shot had been fired. The single casualty had been an FBI agent who had been killed when his car slid off a snowbound road not far from the standoff.

"The prudent thing was to put patience above the risk of bloodshed," said FBI Director Louis Freeh, himself a former FBI agent who had been appointed to head the bureau by President Clinton in 1993. "[But] the law was enforced in Montana. We stayed there until we arrested them. That's a pretty strong message to send to anyone who would break the law."

Crackdown on Drug Cartels

With U.S. and Colombian officials working in concert, a major crackdown on the cartels that control the world's cocaine market has succeeded in putting many drug kingpins behind bars. In mid-1996, President Clinton also signed an executive order designed to stop the flow of illegal money by the Cali cartel, a Colombian-based drug ring that authorities have described as the world's largest. The order prohibits four men identified as leaders of the cartel, 43 associates, and some 33 businesses—including Colombia's largest drug store chain, import-export firms, holding companies, and automobile dealers—from having

access to any assets in the U.S. or doing business with U.S. citizens.

President Clinton also ordered the Justice, State, and Treasury departments and other agencies to jointly "identify and put on notice nations that tolerate money laundering," and forced violators to "bring their banks and financial systems into conformity" with international standards, or face sanctions. Those countries with poor "money laundering" track records include Austria, the Bahamas, Greece, Panama, and Turkey.

Natural Disasters and FEMA

Not often was the failure of a federal agency so total and so obvious.

On August 24, 1992, Hurricane Andrew flattened a 50-mile-wide path of destruction across southern Florida, leaving 200,000 residents homeless and another one million without power. For three long days, the Federal Emergency Management Agency (FEMA)—its primary function is to coordinate federal disaster relief—was nowhere to be found. When FEMA finally did roll into town, its widely reported incompetence

Downtown Clarkesville, Missouri, is underwater from the flooding of the Mississippi River.

delayed and complicated relief efforts further. At FEMA distribution centers—undermanned and ill-equipped—lines for food and water stretched for miles.

FEMA had been created in 1979 to prepare for massive nuclear war with the Soviet Union. Every year, more than half of its annual budget (now just under $1 billion) went to that mission, thereby draining its secondary but far more immediate function of rendering assistance in event of natural disasters.

Three years before Hurricane Andrew hit Florida, FEMA had failed to deliver when Hurricane Hugo smashed Puerto Rico and the U.S. Virgin Islands with winds well in excess of 100 mph. Anticipating a disaster, Puerto Rico's governor quickly requested federal assistance, only to have the forms he submitted returned to him—by regular mail days after Hugo had hit—because he had failed to check off one box on the form. As his homeland was digging out from under its worst hurricane in this century, the governor was forced to refile the forms with FEMA, delaying federal aid.

Time and again, whether it was fires or earthquakes or hurricanes or floods, FEMA seemed determined to live up to the label once tagged on it by Senator Ernest Hollings after a major disaster in his state of South Carolina: "They're the sorriest bunch of bureaucratic jackasses I've ever known."

After FEMA had mishandled relief effort in the 1989 Loma Prieta earthquake in California, Congressman Norman Minetta (D-California), chairman of the oversight committee that keeps an eye on the agency, had said that FEMA could "screw up a two-car parade." In 1993, weeks of nonstop rains caused the Mississippi River and its tributaries to crest far beyond previous records, unleashing floods that isolated or damaged 42,000 homes and displaced 100,000 residents. The entire state of Iowa was declared a federal disaster area, as were sections of eight other Mississippi River border states. Following the Mississippi River flooding, Minetta observed that FEMA had "delivered finally on its promise to stand with the American people when floods or hurricanes or earthquake devastate their communities."

It had taken 12 months to reform and rejuvenate what many observers, in and out of government, believed to be the worst-run federal agency into one of the best. Upon taking office, the President had appointed James Lee Witt as FEMA director. Witt, a former construction firm owner, had proven himself capable when he ran the state of Arkansas's office of emergency services and had ably managed three major natural disasters.

Witt cleaned out upper and middle management at FEMA, which had a much higher ratio of political appointees than most government agencies. The fact that there were a lot of appointive positions, however, helped Witt's cause. He was able to free the agency of all

The 1994 Northridge earthquake (above) and 1989's Hurricane Hugo (right) left billions of dollars in damage and thousands of people in need. Both were answered by FEMA, with widely differing results.

the dead wood—rarely easy in the government sector—and find qualified replacements.

He then determined that, with the Cold War ended and the Soviet Union no more, a massive nuclear attack seemed highly unlikely. So, he shut down that arm of the agency, which freed many resources—people and matériel—that had long been tied up preparing for war with the Soviets.

Within hours of the Oklahoma City bombing, the first advance team from FEMA was on the ground, with damage assessors and high-level members of Witt's staff. Six hours later, Witt arrived to be briefed, and that evening, the first of FEMA's search and rescue teams arrived to help the city's police and fire departments in their rescue efforts. "My office was very happy with the quick response of FEMA," said that city's civil emergency director.

Disaster relief also came in the form of low-interest FEMA loans to individuals (up to $120,000) and businesses (up to $500,000), as well as federal dollars to help local taxpayers bear the cost of a budget-breaking calamity. For example, after the 1994 Northridge earthquake in California, which killed 61 people, injured 5,900 others, and left 20,000 homeless, President Clinton authorized $45 million to remove debris from the shattered highways, $95 million for small-business loans, and $100 million to repair local roads and other facilities. Another $100 million was made available to pay for the rent for displaced low-income families.

When Congressional hearings were held to assess the job being done by the reorganized agency, witnesses including a very grateful Missouri state emergency management director ("our flood showcased FEMA's new commitment and successful efforts in disaster response to catastrophic events") turned the session into a bipartisan love fest seldom seen on Capitol Hill.

"I haven't spent a lot of time complimenting the President on his appointments," admitted Oklahoma Republican Jim Inhofe. "But I sure do on [Witt]."

Even FEMA's longtime most vociferous congressional critic, Senator Barbara Mikulski (D-Maryland), seems to have had a change of opinion, too. She says of FEMA's Witt: "He absolutely gets A's for effort."

Immigration

Immigration Enforcement Improvements Act
(Legislation pending)

The Clinton Administration sent a legislative proposal to Congress in 1995 to strengthen the country's strategy for combatting illegal immigration. [Note: TB trying to find out if this act passed.] This proposed legislation provides for

* No fewer than 700 new Border Patrol agents.

* An Employment Verification Pilot Program to determine the most effective means of removing a significant incentive to illegal immigration: employment in the U.S.

* Increased penalties for alien smuggling, illegal reentry, failure to depart, employer violations, and immigration document fraud.

* Streamlined deportation procedures so that criminal aliens can be more expeditiously removed from the United States.

* New sanctions to be imposed against countries that refuse to accept the deportation of their nationals from the United States.

This effort would complement an earlier 1995 presidential memorandum that directed heads of executive departments and agencies within the federal government to take specific steps to fight illegal immigration, including strengthening border control, intensifying workplace enforcement, and expanding detention and deportation capabilities.

A record 51,600 illegal and criminal aliens were deported in 1995—a 15 percent increase over 1994. Also, the number of Border Patrol agents along the southwestern border was increased by 50 percent in an effort to stem the flow of illegal aliens coming into the United States.

President's Duty: Provide for the Common Defense

With a rapidly changing geopolitical landscape, President Clinton inherited a very different world than his predecessor had just four years before. In 1988, there was still a Soviet Union, an Eastern Bloc, and countless trouble spots throughout the world. While the stakes of a full-scale nuclear confrontation between the world's two superpowers were still incalculably high, that, ironically, had traditionally worked to create a certain stability or balance in the relationship between the U.S. and the Soviet Union.

Then, on President Bush's watch, came the fall of the "Evil Empire" and the end of the Cold War the world had known for a generation. With the dismantling of the Berlin Wall, a new "world order" had been born.

By 1992, Eastern Europe, while finally free of Communist domination, faced new dangers from long dormant ethnic hostilities and nascent sovereignty movements in the Balkans, Chechnya, and Ukraine. Moreover, a very real threat to the U.S. existed as vast arsenals of nuclear missiles, still targeted for U.S. soil, remained physically based in unstable territories in the old Soviet Union. With no identifiable government in place, for a time it was anyone's guess who controlled the warheads.

In the face of these unprecedented challenges, and lacking on-the-job training in foreign affairs, the Clinton Administration was required to chart a course through one potential minefield after another. Their primary goal: continued national security for the U.S. "The new security must seek to bind a broader Europe together," President

Clinton explained, "with a strong fabric woven of military cooperation, prosperous market economies, and vital democracies."

Military Readiness

Nuclear Weapons Reductions

Under the Clinton Administration, START I, an ambitious weapons reduction treaty that reduced U.S. and Russian strategic nuclear weapons by 40 percent, went into effect. After securing Senate ratification of START II, the Clinton Administration was able to put into motion a further 25 percent reduction in each country's nuclear stockpiles.

At the 1994 summit between President Clinton and Russian president Boris Yeltsin, the two leaders hammered out an agreement to accelerate the shrinkage of nuclear arsenals beyond what was called for by the START treaties. By mid-1996, the U.S. had eliminated 750 strategic nuclear missiles, and about 800 strategic nuclear missiles in the former Soviet Union had been eliminated, including more than 700 in Russia. The two countries also agreed to remove enough nuclear missiles from active service to get down to the weapons level specified in START II without waiting until 2003, as the treaty provides. This would remove 5,600 Russian warheads and about half that many U.S. warheads from active duty years ahead of schedule.

The Administration had considered this an urgent matter because Russia's arsenal of tactical weapons was scattered across scores of military sites controlled by local commanders, not by Moscow. This increased the danger that weapons or nuclear materials could be stolen or sold. This "loose nukes" threat was regarded by the Administration as far graver to world peace and U.S. security than the possibility today of a nuclear strike by Russian strategic missiles.

Perhaps the Clinton Administration's most noteworthy defense-related accomplishment during its first term, however, was obtaining a historic agreement with the Russian government to de-target all missiles aimed at the United States. For the first time since the beginning of the Cold War, no Russian nuclear weapons have American cities in their crosshairs.

Ukraine Denuclearization

A high priority of the new administration was to convince Ukraine to give up its ex-Soviet arsenal of some 1,900 strategic nuclear warheads, the world's third largest nuclear stockpile. Most of the warheads sat atop SS-19 and SS-24 Inter-Continental Ballistic Missiles targeted for the U.S.

Secretary of Defense William Perry (third from left) inspects a crater where a destroyed Ukrainian missile silo once stood.

After more than a year of high-level negotiations throughout most of 1993, President Clinton traveled to Kiev, Ukraine, in January 1994 to meet with Ukrainian president Leonid Kravchuk. Ukraine wanted U.S. aid and the U.S. wanted the elimination of Ukraine's nuclear arsenal. The U.S.-Russia-Ukraine Trilateral Statement and Annex was consequently signed by the presidents of all three countries in Moscow on January 14, 1994. The deal provided for the dismantling of all nuclear weapons in Ukraine in exchange for international loans, increased trade, and new foreign aid from the U.S.

On June 1, 1996, President Clinton announced that there were no nuclear weapons left on Ukraine soil, as they had all been decommissioned and disassembled. Similar disarmament agreements were concluded with Kazakhstan and Belarus, other former Soviet republics. As a result, by mid-1996, they were nearly nuclear free.

At the request of the White House, $3 billion was allocated by Congress in a 1995 foreign operations appropriations bill for denuclearization. Another $300 million to dismantle Eastern Bloc nuclear missiles was provided in 1996 through a bipartisan bill carried by Senators Sam Nunn (D-Georgia) and Richard Lugar (R-Indiana).

Conventional Forces Reduction in Europe

After two years of negotiations led by the United States, 30 nations reached a wide-ranging European disarmament agreement in Vienna in June 1996. The Conventional Forces in Europe (CFE) Treaty resolved a problem that had arisen concerning the level of Russian and Ukrainian military equipment allowed on the northern and southern flank of central Europe.

The CFE countries—including Russia, Ukraine, and many Central and Eastern European nations—agreed to cooperate in providing for a new, more stable Europe through the destruction of some 50,000 tanks, armored combat vehicles, artillery pieces, combat aircraft, and attack helicopters. The treaty also established a trust, but verify, system of on-site inspections.

New Democracies

"Ultimately, the best strategy to ensure our security and build a durable peace is to support the advance of democracy," President Clinton told a Joint Session of Congress in 1994. "Democracies do not attack each other; they make better partners in trade and diplomacy."

Not surprising, the Clinton Administration has strongly supported democratic reformers in Russia and in the other states of the former Soviet bloc. Commerce Secretary Ron Brown was the President's leading emissary in helping to build bipartisan support in Congress for initiatives to help Russia, Ukraine, and other newly formed states through epic transformations from dictatorships to democracy.

In 1974, only 39 countries—one in four of the world's independent nations—were democratic. By 1996, a historic number of people were

The inspiring product of another example of newly opened elections and the New Democracies, South African President Nelson Mandela visited the White House in 1994.

selecting their governments by ballot. "Today, five years after the fall of the Soviet Union," reported the *Wall Street Journal* in June 1996, "one hundred and seventeen countries—nearly two of every three independent nations—use open elections to choose their top leaders."

North Korean Nuclear Threat

North Korea was a signatory to the nuclear Non-Proliferation Treaty in 1985 before its first nuclear reactor ever went into operation. Then, once its reactor came on-line, North Korean officials kept delaying required inspections by the International Atomic Energy Agency (IAEA). When inspections were finally allowed, the IAEA found evidence that North Korea was actively pursuing the development of its own nuclear weapons program by acquiring the technology and fissionable material to construct their own bombs. The growing menace of North Korea as a nuclear power in such a volatile region where the U.S. had already fought one war became a serious threat.

In 1993, North Korea suddenly announced that it intended to withdraw from the nuclear Non-Proliferation Treaty, thereby ending the

IAEA's right to inspect its nuclear facilities. Although under intense international pressure North Korea agreed to remain with the treaty's inspection system, it continually resisted IAEA inspections.

Then, in May 1994, North Korea flatly rejected a request from the IAEA to sample and analyze fuel at one of its key nuclear facilities, calling such an inspection "inappropriate." The Clinton Administration threatened the Pyongyang regime with worldwide diplomatic and economic isolation, and firm reminders of America's role should North Korea ever attack South Korea.

Defense Secretary William Perry publicly laid out in stark terms the commitment of the U.S. to defend South Korea if war broke out, and pledged that the combined forces of the two nations "would decisively and rapidly defeat any attack from the North." The U.S. could not afford to do nothing, Perry said, as North Korea proceeded with its nuclear program.

At that point, Perry estimated that North Korea would have enough plutonium to produce five or six nuclear bombs by the end of 1994. In addition to South Korea, there was a potential threat to Japan and Taiwan if North Korea developed delivery systems. "We have to regard the situation as very dangerous," Perry warned.

The Clinton Administration believed that if efforts to halt North Korea's nuclear buildup failed, other renegade states intent on building such weapons could be encouraged to proceed with their programs. North Korea was given two choices: continue its nuclear weapons program and face the consequences, possibly including war, or drop it and accept economic aid and normal relations with the U.S. and its allies.

On June 20, 1994, North Korea responded that it would "never allow inspections" of two suspected nuclear waste sites and warned that sanctions would lead to war. China, an ally of North Korea, upped the ante in announcing its opposition to sanctions.

Nevertheless, the Clinton Administration went forward with plans to put the issue of sanctions before the U.N. Security Council for a vote, as a wary South Korea stepped up civil-preparedness measures.

Three days later, North Korea relented, agreeing to freeze its nuclear program. This was an important first step in resolving the standoff over that country's nuclear weapons program. High-level talks would resume in Geneva between the two countries, aimed at a comprehensive settlement of the North Korean nuclear issue in return for closer diplomatic and economic ties between the U.S. and North Korea.

As a result of the confrontation, North Korea agreed to fully abide by the nuclear Non-Proliferation Treaty, including allowing inspectors access to any of its facilities.

Military Spending

The 1995-96 defense budget—$1.4 billion higher than the previous year's spending—totaled $243 billion. It provided for accelerated procurement of major warships, aircraft, and weapons systems, as well as funds to finance ongoing operations such as peacekeeping in Bosnia, monitoring Iraq's military, and dealing with other trouble spots. Some of the expenditures for hardware included:

- $2.2 billion for development of the F-22, America's next premier fighter aircraft
- $844 million for 18 more FA-18 planes
- $370 million toward development of a national ballistic missile defense system
- $493 million for starting procurement of 1 more B-2 bomber
- $700 million for a third Seawolf submarine
- $700 million for a new attack submarine

While supporting a strong national defense to secure America's role as the "world's peacemaker," President Clinton has nevertheless sought cuts to control unnecessary spending for defense as he has in other areas of government. In mid-1996, the Republican-led Senate and House each passed its own version of the 1996-97 defense appropriations bill that called for $10 billion more than the Clinton Administration wanted.

While supporting his pledge that the "men and women who serve under the American Flag will remain the best-trained, the best-prepared,

and the best-equipped fighting force in the world," he threatened a presidential veto if the $245 billion proposed defense budget wasn't cut. The White House explained that the bill was simply not affordable at a time when the nation faces "serious budget constraints." The results of the bill are pending.

President Clinton meets with the U.S. troops at the air base in Tuzla, Bosnia.

President's Duty: Promote the General Welfare

To effectively promote the general welfare, a U.S. President must execute an agenda with a wide range of issues that greatly impact on Americans in their daily lives. A middle-income, two-parent family with three school-age children in Cincinnati has different day-to-day concerns than a single mother with a baby receiving Medicaid in Atlanta or an unmarried, wealthy Wall Street broker. But to every citizen, the important areas of consideration are the economy, health care, business, and education.

The Economy

When President Clinton took office, 12 years of supply-side or "trickle-down" economics had resulted in an annual federal deficit that was the highest in U.S. history: $290 billion, according to the Congressional Budget Office. More than any other issue, the economy was Bill Clinton's ticket into the White House.

President Reagan, considered the father of supply-side economics, had bet on a combination of big tax cuts and huge defense spendings to stimulate economic growth—with mixed results. On the upside, in trying to match U.S. defense outlays, the Soviet Union went bankrupt, hastening its eventual collapse. At the same time, after an initial expansion "trickle-down" economics caused a slowdown in the U.S. economy. High unemployment, the collapse of the Savings and Loan industry, and rising interest rates fueled a full-blown recession. Between 1989 and 1992, the U.S. economy experienced the slowest growth in a half century. All this led to Presidential candidate Bill Clinton's famous campaign theme, "It's the economy, stupid," and his 1992 victory over incumbent president George Bush.

President Clinton signs into law his Omnibus Budget Reconciliation Act on August 10, 1993.

When President Reagan came into office he had informed the American people that if the national debt was stacked in thousand-dollar bills, the pile would reach 67 miles into space. Unfortunately, there was not a high priority placed on deficit reduction during the Reagan and Bush Administrations, so on the day President Clinton was inaugurated, that same stack of thousand-dollar bills would have reached 267 miles into space. During the Reagan/Bush era, the U.S. had the most rapid increase in annual deficits in this country's history, causing the national debt to quadruple from $1 trillion to $4 trillion. Beginning in 1996, the interest alone on the national debt exceeded, for the first time, the entire defense budget.

By 1992, the public's mandate was clear: turn the economy around now. Furthermore, it made sense to most Americans that the government should be on the same type of budget that virtually every well-run household in the country was on: spend no more than what you bring in.

In the days preceding his inauguration, President Clinton assembled his economic advisors and presented them with a difficult choice. He had been elected on a platform of tax relief for the lower and middle class, faster economic growth, and budget-deficit reductions. Which of the three should be tackled first?

The President and his advisors, cognizant that the strong desire of the American people to right the economy won the election for them, chose deficit-reduction as their number-one priority. President Clinton's economic package presented to Congress in early 1993 included not only specifics for attacking the deficit, but also that year's proposed budget, a budget outline for the next four years, and scores of very detailed initiatives for reviving the American economy.

Omnibus Budget Reconciliation Act of 1993
PL 103 - 66

The Administration's plan for lowering the deficit—the cornerstone of its 1993 economic package—was the subject of a rancorous eight-month political struggle in Congress that cumulated in a 51-50 vote in the Senate with Vice President Al Gore breaking the tie. This act committed the government to reducing the budget deficit by a total of about $500 billion over four years. This would be achieved through cuts in domestic spending totaling about $250 billion (opposed by some Democrats) that eliminated 100 domestic programs and cut spending in more than 300 budget items, and about $250 billion in tax increases (opposed by most Republicans), such as increased taxes on individuals making more than $250,000 a year and a four-cent boost in federal gasoline taxes.

"This plan has already begun to work," President Clinton said in ceremonies on the South Lawn of the White House when he signed the budget act. "Ever since it was clear that we were working to bring down the deficit and every time we made progress along the way, long-term interest rates dropped, enabling millions of Americans to refinance their homes, either to lower their monthly payments or to build up their own savings, and enabling businesses to refinance their loans."

Although money markets around the world reacted positively, the political fallout over the President's deficit-reduction package and his overall budget plan did not immediately disappear. "I believe this will lead to a recession next year," Representative Newt Gingrich (R-Georgia) predicted. "This is the Democratic machine's recession, and each one of them will be held personally accountable."

"We're going to find out whether we have higher deficits," echoed

Representative John Kasich, a leading Republican. "We're going to find out whether we have a slower economy. We're going to find out what's going to happen to interest rates. And it's our bet that this is a job killer."

Critics, however, were proved wrong. The deficit went from $290 billion the day President Clinton stepped foot in the White House to $130 billion by 1996. For the first time in 150 years, the U.S. Government's deficit went down four consecutive years under the same Administration.

For average Americans, this resulted in the lowest combined rate of unemployment, inflation, and mortgage interest rates in 27 years. Because interest rates were down, business investment in equipment grew at seven times the pace of the previous four years. Auto sales went way up, with U.S.-made automobiles outselling imports. Home sales hit near-record highs—4.22 million sales in April 1996 was the second best ever recorded. Not only has the nation's gross national product steadily expanded over the last three and a half years, but over 10 million new jobs have been created, a faster annual rate of job growth than any Republican Administration since the 1920s.

President Clinton accomplished many of his economic goals his first two years in office, when he was able to work with a Democratic-controlled Congress. That is not to say, however, that he did not fight very public battles with members of his own party. Unlike in other Democratic Administrations, inflation and increased interest rates did not occur as expected. The reason it did not happen this time was because of the new President's commitment to reducing the deficit—a seemingly "un-Democratic" course to follow, but one that the voters had made clear should be a top priority. As a result, interest rates went down and inflation was nowhere to be seen, both of which helped rev up the economy.

The end result was that President Clinton found himself during his first term presiding over the largest peacetime economic expansion in history. As for increasing taxes, both the *Wall Street Journal* and H&R Block agreed that only 1.2 percent of American taxpayers (those earning $250,000 or more a year) had their taxes increased by the President's plan. The vast majority of Americans had their taxes lowered.

The President's plan resulted in steady economic growth. According to the latest figures from the Commerce Department, the U.S. economy is continuing to expand—at a rate of 2.8 percent during the first quarter of 1996 and 4.2 percent during the second quarter. Another significant result of this expansion: 1.28 million fewer people are on welfare rolls today than when President Clinton took office, an 8 percent decline.

Minimum Wage Act
Included in Small Business Job Protection Act of 1996
HR 3448
Sponsor: Rep. Bill Archer (R-Texas)

The U.S. first adopted a minimum wage during the depths of the Depression in 1938. The initial hourly minimum wage was 25 cents an hour. Throughout much of the postwar era, the minimum wage hovered around half the average wage. But as of 1996, it was just over a third of the average wage. It had remained stuck at $4.25 an hour, with no increase since 1991. Today, 60 percent of minimum wage workers are women. More than a third are the sole breadwinners in their household. Over two million children live in poor or near-poor families where a worker earns a minimum wage.

The issue cut cleanly along party lines. While many Republicans opposed any increase at all, every one of the 47 Democrats in the Senate favored the 90 cents an hour increase asked for by the Administration. There was much political wrangling—Democrats held out for a "clean" vote on minimum wage alone, while Republicans sought to gut the wage bill by tying it to reduction in Welfare eligibility.

Eventually, in July 1996, after considerable election-year rhetoric on both sides, the bill passed the Senate in a 74-to-24—the result of a unified Democratic front and deep cracks within the Republican ranks. President Clinton acknowledged it had been a difficult fight. He characterized the wage increase as a "real victory" for millions of hard-working people and families. At the same time, he beseeched Congress for a bipartisan commitment to ensure that the minimum wage be allowed to keep better pace with the cost of living.

Welfare Reform

Begun as a federal entitlement program to provide temporary financial assistance to citizens unable to earn a livable income, welfare has been a volatile political issue for many years. Democrats have traditionally acted as guardians of the program and Republicans have repeatedly called for its abolition. Most seem to be in agreement, however, that the current system is now at the point of being a big part of the problem it was originally intended to help solve. Far from helping to fight poverty, it has instead helped create an "underclass" by removing incentives for many to get legitimate employment because welfare benefits outweigh the benefits derived from low-paying jobs.

After rancorous debate in both houses of Congress, historic welfare reform legislation was passed in late July 1996, and is expected to be signed into law by President Clinton in early August. The following are key provisions of the bill:

• States will have until July 1, 1997, to submit plans for new programs to replace Aid to Families With Dependent Children, the federal program that guarantees cash assistance for poor children.

• Each state will now receive a lump sum to run its own welfare and work programs.

• Lifetime welfare benefits will be limited to five years, with hardship exemptions available for 20 percent of families.

• The head of each family on welfare must work within two years or lose benefits.

• States can provide benefits to unmarried teenage parents under 18 years old only if the mother stays in school and lives with an adult.

• Food stamps will be limited for adults with no dependent children.

• Legal immigrants would not receive most benefits during their first five years in the U.S.

• States must provide Medicaid for all who qualify under the current law.

Health Care

Family Medical Leave Act
PL 103 - 03
Sponsor: Rep. William D. Ford (D-Michigan)

The first bill signed by President Clinton after he had been in office only one month had previously been vetoed by President George Bush. This law covers 60 percent of the nation's workforce at 5 percent of the nation's employers—those with 50 or more employees—allowing more than 42 million working Americans to take up to 12 weeks of unpaid leave when facing a medical or health crisis, or to care for a sick family member or a new child without fear of losing their jobs. It is estimated as many as 2.5 million workers will benefit from such unpaid leaves every year. A reported 12 million people have already taken advantage of the law. Key employees, identified as those who are among the highest paid 10 percent of a company's workforce, are not subject to the act.

The Family Medical Leave Act had been twice vetoed by President Bush, but signed into law by President Clinton on February 5, 1993.

Republican opposition at the time suggested that allowing unpaid leaves would be costly to business. However, the Conference Board, a pro-business group, recently reported that 70 percent of employers said complying with the new law was "easy" or "very easy." And a bipartisan commission on leave said that 9 out of 10 companies involved said the act did not cost them any money or have any negative impact on their profits.

In June 1996, President Clinton proposed that Congress expand Family Leave to allow employees to also take up to 24 hours a year for

parent-teacher conferences or for routine medical care for a child, a spouse, or a partner. Congressional action on this request has not yet been taken.

Health Care Security Act of 1993

For six decades, many Administrations have attempted to enact health care reform. President Roosevelt tried. President Truman tried. President Nixon tried. President Carter tried. A cornerstone of candidate Bill Clinton's campaign had been his pledge to establish a form of national health care for everyone. Upon entering the White House, the issue became, after deficit reduction, the President's second biggest domestic priority.

Eyebrows were raised when the job of coordinating the Administration's Health Care Task Force was given to First Lady Hillary

First Lady Hillary Rodham Clinton, the Administration's coordinator on health care, meets with sick children and children with ill family members who need insurance.

First Lady Hillary Rodham Clinton appears before the Senate Finance Committee to discuss health care reform and argue the Administration's position on reform.

Rodham Clinton. This surprise appointment initially won broad praise—she was publicly complimented by congressional leaders from both parties for her grasp of the issue and her articulate call for reform, and no less than the *New York Times* dubbed her "St. Hillary" in a cover story in its Sunday magazine. But after a $100 million opposition lobbying campaign and a failure to build a broad enough base of political support, the effort to pass the Act dissolved in contention and disarray on Capitol Hill in what marked the biggest legislative setback of Bill Clinton's presidency.

From the beginning of the Administration's efforts, there was little partisan consensus in Congress on health care reform. The President and Democratic legislators stated they would accept only a proposal with coverage available for every single American, while Republicans did not want a policy that required employers to provide insurance. The public was divided as well. While most Americans favored health care for all, they didn't want to pay higher taxes to achieve it or be forced into managed-care programs.

The Clinton Administration's health care reform program sought to provide universal coverage—with built-in cost controls—to all Americans by requiring employers to buy private insurance or pay into a public system. The White House sought to address some of the concerns from the business community by including a number of features designed to ease the impact on business—phasing in benefit requirements for small businesses until costs were reduced, and allowing small employers to pool together to receive more favorable rates from insurers.

The plan failed to pass in Congress for numerous reasons. Critics claimed that it would cost too much and lead to government bureaucratic interference in the health care system. Other detractors said that instead of focusing only on a managed-competition plan as a way to lower premiums—a strategy that would have had a better chance of gaining bipartisan support—the Administration erred by not ruling out a single-payer plan for universal coverage, which would have put the U.S. government in the health care business.

Republican critics charged that Representative Newt Gingrich (R-Georgia) was convinced that Republicans would win control of Congress in 1994 by denying the Clinton Administration any sort of legislative victory on health care. But leading Democrats, such as Senator Daniel Patrick Moynihan (D-New York), thought the plan too ambitious and politically unattainable. The health care industry was divided into opposing groups that consisted of smaller independent insurers, hospitals, and doctors who felt threatened by the proposed sweeping changes and lobbied hard against its passage, while the larger insurance companies favoring managed competition tended to support it.

White House insiders later commented that another possible reason for defeat was that the Administration failed to give the public a clear sense of how the plan was supposed to work. They claimed its message—that universal coverage would in fact lower health care costs in the long run—never came across to the American people.

"We probably should have gone at health care more slowly, and more incrementally," admitted George Stephanopoulos, senior advisor to the President. He said they should have taken the time to explain it better to the American people, "instead of trying to rush it through."

With the defeat of the President's health care reform, public skepticism toward the Clinton Administration reached a peak in 1994, when Congress was captured—as Gingrich had hoped—by a Republican majority in both the Senate and House. But the issue of health care reform did not go away, and remained a part of the national debate to be addressed with later legislation.

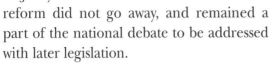

The Child Immunization Act, signed into law on April 20, 1994, gave millions of children access to free immunization clinics (below).

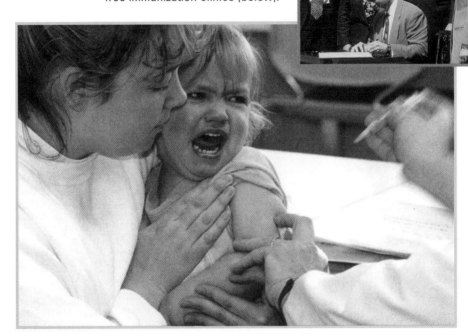

Comprehensive Child Immunization Initiative

Established by President Clinton in 1994, this program—the first of its kind—assures that all children in the U.S., regardless of income, are guaranteed to receive a complete schedule of inoculations and

vaccinations. This initiative establishes a national tracking system through grants to the states to establish state immunization registries to ensure that children receive their scheduled immunizations at the earliest appropriate age. In 1995, the immunization rate for two-year-old children reached 75 percent, an all-time high.

The President used many different public occasions to bring attention to women's health issues.

Women, Infants and Children's Nutrition Program

This program was expanded under the Clinton Administration, with funding increased $610 million through 1995, a 21 percent jump. As a result, it is estimated that an additional one million disadvantaged women and children in the U.S. were able to get the nutrition they needed to stay healthy.

Breast Cancer Research

As part of his 1993 economic package, the President secured a 65 percent increase in National Institutes of Health funding for breast cancer research.

Children and Tobacco

The Clinton Administration announced in mid-1995 a comprehensive plan to reduce smoking by children and adolescents by 50 percent through stronger efforts to reduce access to tobacco products and limit its appeal for minors. Specifically, the proposal would:

• Require age verification and face-to-face sales, eliminating vending machines, self-service displays, free samples, mail-order sales, packages with fewer than 20 cigarettes ("kiddie packs"), and sale of single cigarettes.

• Ban outdoor advertising of tobacco products within 1,000 feet of schools and playgrounds, and permit black-and-white text only in all other outdoor advertising.

• Prohibit brand-name sponsorship of sporting or entertainment events.

• Require the tobacco industry to fund ($150 million annually) a public education campaign to prevent children from smoking. The bill has not yet been acted upon by Congress.

New System for Testing Meats

The 1993 epidemic of food poisoning in the Pacific Northwest that afflicted 500 people and killed five children brought attention to the inadequate methods being used by the USDA in examining and approving meats for public consumption. In July 1996, the President issued an executive order, not requiring congressional approval, to improve the nation's federal meat inspection system—largely unchanged since the early 1900s. The order called for a new system to guard against deadly bacteria in meat and poultry by relying more on scientific testing and less on the touch, sight, and smell of federal inspectors.

The responsibility for designing and implementing the new system—expected to take several months to roll out—and footing its cost of perhaps $100 million will fall mainly on private industry. Under the plan, slaughterhouses and meatpackers will also be required to come up with new, scientific methods of preventing contamination. Agricultural Department inspectors will be required to approve each plant's program and verify its effectiveness. Plants that fail to implement a satisfactory program could be penalized and even closed down.

Health Coverage Availability and Affordability Act of 1996

HR 3103
Sponsors: Sen. Nancy Kassebaum (R-Kansas) and Sen. Edward Kennedy (D-Massachusetts)

As a result of the continuing debate raised during the Administration's attempt to pass the Health Care Security Act of 1993, the Kennedy-Kassebaum bill was designed to help workers and families retain health coverage when they change or lose jobs, or have preexisting medical conditions. Passed in both houses of Congress, the Act:

• Calls for the complete elimination of preexisting conditions as grounds for insurance companies to deny coverage to applicants.

• Addresses the issue of affordability.

• Recommends the implementation of cost controls.

• Prohibits insurance companies from denying coverage to workers when they change jobs.

• Helps individuals who have lost their job maintain coverage.

President Clinton strongly backed the measure in his 1996 State of the Union address, and is expected to sign it into law.

Business

Tax Cut for Small Businesses

The Clinton Administration's 1993 economic package created new tax cuts for 9 out of 10 small businesses in the country. This was accomplished by increasing from $10,000 to $17,500 per year the amount small businesses and self-employed individuals can deduct for purchasing depreciable assets, including computers, electronic equipment, and other items used for business purposes. This 75 percent increase in the "expensing limit" was something that the small business community had sought unsuccessfully for years. The Treasury Department has estimated that 1.3 million small businesses will benefit from the provision in 1996. As part of its 1993 economic package, the Clinton Administration also:

• Enacted a 50 percent capital-gains tax exclusion targeted at investments in small businesses by allowing investors who buy newly issued stock in small businesses and hold that stock for more than five years to receive a 50 percent cut in the capital-gains tax on the profit from the sale of the stock.

• Supported private investment by securing a three-year extension of the tax credit for business research and development, retroactive to June 1992, and effective through mid-1995.

Tax breaks and lower interest rates have caused business investments to grow by 11 percent a year since 1993, reported the *New Yorker* (6/10/96)—"the highest rate of growth since the Kennedy Administration."

Telecommunications Act
PL 104 - 104
Sponsor: Sen. Larry Pressler (R-South Dakota)

On February 8, 1996, President Clinton signed the first major overhaul of telecommunications law in almost 62 years. The goal of this new law is to let anyone enter the communications business, protect consumers from monopolies, and promote competition among TV and radio stations, cable operators, and telephone companies. It is hoped to positively affect telephone service (local and long distance), cable programming, and other video and broadcast services.

The law also provides for schools, libraries, and hospitals to receive telecommunications services at reduced costs. It also requires television manufacturers to provide "V-chips" for all new sets so that parents can block certain programming, thereby giving them the ability to protect their children from television violence and other age-inappropriate broadcasts.

The President signed NAFTA into law on December 8, 1993, opening up the opportunities for U.S. businesses to form production partnerships with Mexico and Canada.

North American Free Trade Agreement
PL 103 - 182
Sponsor: Rep. Dan Rostenkowski (D-Illinois)

During the last few decades, the U.S. increasingly faced fierce competition in the area of trade. This stemmed primarily from other countries forming production partnerships to produce goods at more competitive prices. Recognizing that the U.S. economy does not stand on its own but is a major cog in an ever-evolving global economy, President Clinton, despite intense opposition from his own party, forged a bipartisan coalition to pass NAFTA in his first year in office. NAFTA allows businesses in the United States to form production partnerships with Mexico and Canada.

This trade agreement began life as a Republican initiative, and was vigorously opposed by many, especially presidential candidate Ross

Perot, who perceived it as undermining the labor base of the American worker. The reality was an increase in big U.S. companies sending more work overseas where wages were lower and working condition requirements were less stringent. Not only was the U.S. losing jobs, but tax dollars as well. The President stated that NAFTA would not only save jobs, but also open new markets for U.S. products in North America.

NAFTA came under very heavy fire at home, with concerns that U.S. manufacturing plants would close, jobs would be lost, wages would fall, and U.S. economic growth would slow. Perot's vivid discourse on that "sucking sound you hear is all the jobs heading south of the border" resonated from coast to coast. Ironically, the turning point in the debate came when Vice President Al Gore handily proved the Administration's case against Perot on *Larry King Live*.

Leading indicators point out that the codifying production partnerships have produced favorable results for the U.S. economy. "NAFTA is still young, but evidence is trickling in and it's positive for jobs and wages," reported the *Washington Post* (3/5/96). "It is also evident that our economy's growth rate has been affected positively." The Commerce Department estimates that a net of 236,000 new jobs in the U.S. is directly attributable to expanding North American trade over the past two years. The gain of new jobs over displaced jobs is five to one.

"With a favorable disparity on export-related wages," the *Post* continued, "it is clear that NAFTA has been positive for wages. U.S. exports to Mexico and Canada grew at a rate of nearly 20 percent over the past two years—much higher than the overall U.S. export growth rate." With Mexican trade barriers lowered—Mexico lowered its trade barriers 400 percent more than the U.S. did—the U.S. market share of Mexico's imports is up. By the year 2000, all tariffs will be phased out.

General Agreement on Tariffs and Trade
PL 103 - 4560
Sponsor: Rep. Richard Gephardt (D-Missouri)

President Clinton signed the Uruguay Round Agreement Act into law in late 1994. This trade agreement lowers tariffs worldwide by $744

billion over the next 10 years—the largest international reduction in history—and creates a new international trade regime called the World Trade Organization. Significantly, URAA did not cause any dramatic lowering of U.S. barriers to foreign trade, as the U.S. has been the world's most open market for half a century. What URAA did (and NAFTA, too) was primarily open foreign markets to U.S. goods.

American goods and services are uniformly competitive in the world marketplace. As such, the U.S. benefits more than other nations when barriers are lowered. Whenever foreign markets open, as they did with NAFTA and GATT, U.S. exports accelerate—a vital component to America's financial prosperity.

Education

Student Loan Reform Act
Title IV of the Omnibus Budget Reconciliation Act of 1993
Signed by President Clinton, this bill reformed a very inefficient system for making college student loans that had been administered by the individual states. As a result of this act, students now apply directly to the federal government, cutting down on application paperwork and enabling applicants to pay lower loan fees. It is not only easier to get a loan through this centralized system, but the rate of default has declined with flexible payment plans that can be spread out after graduation, based on an individual's income. The streamlining process allowed 20 million borrowers to consolidate all their school loans into one direct loan to be paid back to the federal government at single-digit interest rates.

Pell Grants
The Clinton Administration supported the Pell Grant program, and in 1996 worked to increase the maximum Pell Grant by 12 percent to its highest level ever: $2,620.

The President's new budget would increase annual funding every year ($3.4 billion by 2002)—enough to reach 960,000 more disadvantaged students in need of financial assistance to meet college costs and increase the maximum award to $3,128.

Goals 2000: The Educate America Act
PL 103 - 227
Sponsor: Rep. Dale E. Kildee (D-Michigan)

Goals 2000: The Educate America Act offers grants to states that commit to education reforms.

Signed into law by the President, this act has set up national educational goals and offers grants to states that commit themselves to reforms. Its eight goals are as follows:

- All students start school ready to learn.
- At least 90 percent of students graduate from high school.
- Students demonstrate competence in basic subjects before passing through grades 4, 8, and 12.
- Teachers have access to continuing education.
- The U.S. will become the highest-ranked nation in math and science achievement.
- All adults will be literate and possess the skills needed to compete in a global economy.
- Schools are free of drugs and violence.
- Each school promotes parental involvement.

Rick Hetzel works as an apprentice at Eastman Kodak as a result of the School-to-Work Act.

To achieve these goals, the bill provides for $400 million to be passed on to the states in the form of grants to be used as the individual states see fit. Since 1994, 48 states have received Goals 2000 funding.

In his 1996 budget, President Clinton called for nearly doubling the funding for the program, to almost $700 million—with the level rising to $896 million by 2002. That amount is estimated to be enough to support improvements for all 44 million school children in more than 85,000 public schools.

School-to-Work Opportunities Act
PL 103 - 239
Sponsor: Rep. William D. Ford (D-Michigan)

This landmark legislation, signed into law by President Clinton in 1994, provides funding to facilitate a nationwide system designed to help America's young people progress more smoothly from a high school classroom to a job with a future. Under this act, schools for the first time are linked to the world of work, with at least one year of apprenticeship being provided beyond high school. The students targeted by this program are the 70 percent of young Americans who don't get four-year college degrees.

Since 1994, the federal government has handed out $320 million in school-to-work grants to 50 states and dozens of communities. In his 1996 budget, President Clinton proposed increasing support by 60 percent to

$400 million, bringing to 43 the number of states implementing school-to-work programs.

"School-to-work has the potential to make an enormous impact on our schools," said Don Davies, founder of the Institute for Responsive Education at Northeastern University in Boston. "It presses schools to improve weak academic programs. And, if taken seriously, it will be a program that for the first time helps all students, not just vocational students, think about what they want to do with their lives."

Under current legislation, School-to-Work would expire in 2001. Some school administrators are already unsure if the programs can be sustained without federal assistance.

A Republican-sponsored bill now before a House-Senate conference committee threatens to repeal the act as early as 1996.

National Service Act
PL 103 - 82
Sponsor: Rep. Matthew Martinez (D-California)

A pet project that President Clinton signed into law in 1993, this act funded AmeriCorps for volunteers to serve communities on a host of levels—tutoring students, immunizing children, reclaiming parks, and patrolling streets—in return for educational stipends toward college or job training, or to repay student loans.

To date, 45,000 AmeriCorps volunteers

Eighth graders view the World Wide Web on a giant monitor during a NetDay demonstration.

have served in schools, hospitals, churches, homeless shelters, and courts. Funding for 1996 is $400 million.

NetDay

The Clinton Administration announced in early 1996 its goal of wiring every classroom in America to the information superhighway by the year 2000. In this instance, the federal government is not footing the entire bill. Rather, a $50 million federal investment in 1996 is expected to draw hundreds of millions of dollars in private support from computer and software manufacturers so that schoolchildren can benefit from computers, software, and trained instructors.

This national effort to wire schoolrooms to the Internet kicked off in June 1996, in California, where thousands of volunteers came in on a Saturday morning and helped wire 3,500 schools, more than a third of the state's total. Among those lending a hand and rolling up their sleeves: President Clinton and Vice President Gore.

The effort has already expanded to two dozen other states, half of which are expected to hold their own NetDay in the fall of 1996.

Head Start

A legacy of President Lyndon Johnson's Great Society, this program to better prepare disadvantaged children for school has long been a success. When President Clinton entered the White House, Head Start was reaching just barely over one-third of all eligible children. Under the Clinton Administration, Head Start funding was increased $760 million from 1993 to 1995, allowing this preschool program to increase the number of children served from 621,000 in 1992 to approximately 840,000 in 1995. The Administration has also reformed the way the program works to improve teaching and facilities.

School Reconstruction

In July 1996, President Clinton announced that he would ask Congress for $5 billion to expand the federal government's role in repairing public schools. If enacted, for the first time, the federal government would join with states and communities to modernize and renovate public schools. The federal funds, together with investments by states and localities, would result in $20 billion in new resources for school modernization over the next four years.

According to White House officials, the Administration's proposal was prompted by General Accounting Office reports over the last year and a half that found $112 billion in pressing school construction needs, including sagging roofs and cracked foundations. In passage of the Education Infrastructure Act of 1994, Congress had approved grants totaling $100 million to build, repair, and renovate school buildings, but the funds were eliminated during budget-balancing negotiations the following year.

President Clinton's proposed school construction initiative would allow for local flexibility, giving communities and states the power to decide where and how to use the new resources. It would, however, focus on sparking new projects, not merely subsidizing existing ones.

A teacher instructs four-year-old children at an Atlanta Head Start Program. During the Clinton Administration Head Start funding increased by over $760 million.

President's Duty: Secure the Blessings of Liberty to Ourselves and Our Posterity

Liberty is about protecting personal rights and freedoms, which are easy to take for granted in 20th century America until they are lost. These fundamental tenets of modern democracy include the citizenry's access to an open and fair political process, its ability to practice its religions of choice with no recrimination, fair opportunities for all, a voice in the reform of government agencies, and the chance to take advantage of all the government has to offer.

Citizens' Rights and Liberties

The President and House Speaker Thomas Foley celebrate enactment of Motor Voter, which enabled 11 million eligible new voters to register.

National Voter Registration Act of 1993
PL 103 - 31
Sponsor: Rep. Al Swift (D-Washington)

In May 1993, President Clinton signed a bill popularly known as the "Motor Voter Act." He had promised during his campaign of 1992 to push for passage of this bill, which began its legislative life as House Resolution 2, but was met with rigorous opposition from Republican lawmakers who had attempted to block it.

As of 1993, it was estimated that 70 million Americans—35 percent of otherwise eligible voters in the U.S.—were not registered to vote. Failure to register was the primary reason given for not voting. This new law, which allows citizens to register at the time they apply for or renew their driver's license as well as through the mail and at various agencies designated by the states, has resulted in an estimated 11 million new registered voters—the greatest expansion of the voter registration rolls since the 19th century.

Lobbying Disclosure Act of 1995
PL 104 - 65
Sponsor: Sen. Carl Levin (D-Michigan)

After two years of Congressional gridlock, President Clinton on December 19, 1995, signed into law this act, which he said would "bring lobbying in Washington into the sunlight of public scrutiny." The previous year, when lobbying reform legislation had been filibustered into oblivion, worried lobbyists who crowded outside the Senate Chamber literally cheered its defeat. This disclosure act, said the President, "is something for the American people to cheer about."

In the first change of rules governing lobbyists since 1946, the new law requires professional lobbyists for the first time to disclose publicly who they are, for whom they work, how much money they're spending, and what bills they're trying to pass, kill or amend. In an earlier lobbying reform initiative, President Clinton, shortly after he had come into office, implemented the toughest ethics code on executive branch officials in history. Henceforth, senior appointees are barred from lobbying their own agencies for five years after leaving office, and from ever lobbying for foreign governments.

Line-Item Veto

PL 104 - 130
Sponsors: Sen. Robert Dole (R-Kansas) and Rep. Bill Archer (R-Texas)

In April 1996, President Clinton signed the Line-Item Veto Act into law, giving a U.S. President the authority to remove specific spending items from bills: new entitlement spending, appropriations spendings, and tax benefits with limited eligibility.

Enactment of the historic measure capped a 12-year effort that started when President Reagan asked Congress for the line-item veto. Only after Republicans took over Congress and it became part of their "Contract with America" was the idea enthusiastically supported. Even so, there was considerable delay and a key provision by the Republican-controlled Congress not to provide the veto and the enormous leverage it wields to President Clinton during the bulk of his first term. The line-item veto goes into effect January 1, 1997.

Beginning in 1997, a President will no longer be in the position of having to reject an entire bill he may otherwise wish to sign because there are a few objectionable line items. With the line-item veto, the President has the ability to eliminate specific line spendings. Congress will then have 30 days to accept the President's decision or pass the offensive spending provisions again by majority vote. If this happens and the offending line items remain intact, the President can veto Congress's action again. Overriding this second veto would take a two-thirds vote in Congress—a difficult achievement in the best of circumstances.

Food and Drug Administration Reform

Through complex and lengthy clinical testing requirements by the slow-moving FDA, Americans have occasionally been denied potential lifesaving medicines that were often available overseas. This "drug lag" had long gone to the heart of the effort for FDA reform. As Congressional debate swirled around legislative proposals that would require the FDA to move faster in ruling on new drugs, the Clinton Administration acted by executive order with several of its own initiatives.

At the behest of the Administration, the FDA first accelerated approval and access to drugs for various AIDS treatments. In one case, the FDA approved ritonavir just 72 days after the manufacturer, Abbott Laboratories, had submitted its application and less than 24 hours after an advisory panel recommended approval. Then, on March 29, 1996, President Clinton announced that his Administration would make the same effort to ensure that anticancer drugs are sped to the market.

"Perhaps more than any other health statistic in America," the President said in a White House ceremony that included several cancer survivors, "cancer touches virtually every family." He added that both his mother and stepfather died of the disease.

That same day FDA Commissioner David Kessler promised that his agency would strive to give quicker approval to drugs that already had been approved in other countries. Pharmaceutical companies would be encouraged to submit to the FDA the same information that made possible the approval abroad. "Whenever possible," Kessler said, "we will use this as the basis for making such therapy available under our expanded access programs to critically ill patients in this country."

Clinics Access Law
PL 103 - 259
Sponsor: Sen. Edward M. Kennedy (D-Massachusetts)

This bill signed into law by President Clinton amends the Public Health Services Act to permit individuals to have freedom of access to certain medical clinics and facilities, including abortion clinics.

Diversity

Religious Freedom Restoration Act

At the time he signed this act in 1993, President Clinton told a Virginia high school audience that it was "one of the proudest things I've been able to do as President." According to the President, it was designed to reverse the decision of the Supreme Court that essentially made it easier for government, in the pursuit of its legitimate objectives, to restrict the exercise of people's religious liberties. "With this Act, we made it possible in areas that were previously ambiguous," he went on, "for Native Americans, American Jews, and Muslims to practice the full range of their religious practices when they might have otherwise come in contact with some governmental regulation."

From now on, the government will have to "bend over backwards to avoid getting in the way of people's legitimate exercise of their religious convictions," the President promised.

Church Burnings

A rash of suspicious fires destroyed black churches in 1995. By mid-1996, at least 40 houses of worship—most in southern states—had been destroyed or damaged by the blazes. Two hundred federal agents were assigned to work with local authorities to investigate the crimes. By June 1996, they had closed 10 cases through arrests and prosecutions, and were working 33 active cases of church arson. Attorney General Janet Reno reported there was no evidence of a conspiracy by arsonists, "but there is clear evidence of racism."

By July 1996, both houses of Congress had passed legislation—422-0 in the House—giving the federal government greater jurisdiction to investigate and prosecute arson at religious buildings, as well as doubling the jail term for church arson from 10 to 20 years. President Clinton promised to sign the bill as soon as it arrived on his desk.

In an effort to prevent further church burnings, the President also authorized an emergency transfer of $6 million to communities in 12

A rash of fires incinerated black churches such as the Rising Star Baptist Church in Greensboro, Alabama (above).

targeted states to hire new police officers, pay overtime for existing officers, hire private security guards, and install floodlights to protect church property. In addition, the President asked FEMA's James Witt to take the lead in working with law enforcement to find ways to stop the burnings before they happen, and to give communities the tools needed to help in the prevention effort.

Of the church burnings, the President said, "This tears at the very heart of what it means to be an American. This has got to stop."

Affirmative Action

In June 1995, the Supreme Court set a new legal standard for judging affirmative action. It ruled that any program that used race, ethnicity, or gender as a consideration to expand opportunity or provided benefits to members of groups that had previously suffered discrimination was ordered eliminated or reformed if it created a quota, created preferences for unqualified individuals, created reverse discrimination, or continued even after its equal opportunity purposes had been achieved.

Some weeks earlier, President Clinton had ordered his staff to conduct a review of all federal affirmative action programs and to ask agencies a number of specific questions about programs that made race or sex a condition of eligibility for any kind of benefit. After the high court's decision, this review was expanded to contain an analysis of the court's decision and its implications for the federal government's hiring policies.

In July 1995, the Administration issued its evaluation of affirmative action in government. Emphasizing a commitment to the "vigorous, effective enforcement of laws prohibiting discrimination," the White House concurred with the findings of the Supreme Court while it reiterated that equality, opportunity, and fair play must be extended to all Americans, regardless of race, ethnicity, or gender. The Administration, in essence, took a mend-it-don't-end-it position on affirmative action, recognizing that it benefited not only ethnic minorities but women in the workplace as well.

Seniors: Medicare Select Expansion

In July 1995, President Clinton signed into law an expansion of the Medicare Select program from 15 states to all 50 states. This program provides for seniors and other qualified Medicare recipients to buy discounted "Medigap" policies through health maintenance organizations and other managed-care providers as long as the patients agree to use the doctors and locations in the plan's network. "Medigap" policies cover the difference between what Medicare pays and what health care costs.

Initially, the White House had expressed concerns about expanding the program—which began in 1990 as a three-year experiment—nationwide before the Department of Health and Human Services finished an ongoing review of its effectiveness. But when the final version of the bill included a provision for reevaluation if studies show it is not cost-effective or diminishes the quality of health care, the Administration was satisfied.

Most of the Medicare Select programs offer beneficiaries premiums at a rate that is 5–10 percent lower than other supplemental Medicare

insurance policies. As of mid-1995, about 450,000 seniors had bought such policies.

Seniors: Increasing the Value of Their Homes

The Department of Housing and Urban Development (HUD) moved in June 1996 to expand a pilot program allowing older Americans to use the value of their homes to supplement their incomes. Under HUD's "reverse mortgage" program, individuals more than 62 years of age who own their homes with no outstanding mortgage can draw against the houses' equity in regular payments. The loan doesn't have to be repaid until the borrower moves out or dies. Banks offering these reverse mortgages are insured against losses by HUD's Federal Housing Authority.

The pilot program had been limited to 50,000 participants. Because of its success and the popularity of reverse mortgages with seniors, HUD asked Congress to revoke the cap and open the program to more than 12 million Americans over age 62 who have fully paid their mortgages. Clinton Administration officials don't expect much Congressional resistance to the expansion, as little financial outlay is required by the federal government.

A Cornell University study estimated that more than 620,000 older Americans could raise themselves above the poverty level by obtaining income based on their home values.

President's Duty: Serve as Commander-in-Chief

Since the fall of the Soviet Union five years ago, the world's sole remaining superpower is the United States. America's role in the world at large has long been a contentious topic at home, with the whirling vortex of the debate pulling in many U.S. Presidents. Invariably, there is a segment of the population that favors an isolationist, "Fortress America" line of foreign policy which places a premium on the national interests of the United States to the virtual exclusion of the rest of the world. Others believe just as strongly that as the "moral" leader of the free world, the U.S. must play the role of global policeman, intervening in hot spots outside its borders to protect and vindicate the rights and interests of people who cannot help themselves.

If anything, this responsibility presents the U.S. with more, not less, difficult choices and decisions than in the old days of the Cold War, when images and loyalties appeared less blurred. Foreign relations are growing more complex by the day, with global financial markets virtually interdependent, and yesterday's enemies turning into today's favored trading partners.

Foreign Affairs

The Nuclear Threat

The threat of nuclear destruction has been greatly reduced thanks, in part, to the START I and II treaties and the de-targeting of Russian

Russian President Boris Yeltsin and Bill Clinton agreed to speed up implementation of the second START agreement, thereby quickening the pace of nuclear disarmament.

missiles. There have been, however, other nuclear-deterrent initiatives put forth by the Clinton Administration. These include the following:

• Increasing U.S. funding to the International Atomic Energy Commission, a watchdog agency that monitors the development, trafficking, and proliferation of nuclear weapons and materials throughout the world. New funds have gone for more inspectors and additional high-tech hardware, and resulted in a 33 percent increase in safeguarding efforts to keep a wary eye on the nuclear programs of Iraq, Libya, and North Korea, as well as the relatively unstable former Soviet republics of Ukraine, Belarus, and Kazakhstan to ensure they are living up to their nuclear disarmament agreements.

• Taking steps to sanction countries that seek to circumvent international guidelines on the transfer of nuclear technology. In 1993, for instance, to protest China's export of ballistic missile parts to Pakistan, the U.S. held up export to China of three U.S.-made communications satellites that the Chinese planned to launch into orbit on their own rockets. In 1994, China again was sanctioned, along with Pakistan, for missile sales to Libya, as was one of the newly formed Russian republics for arms sales to Iran. At the same time, the Administration recognized that nations in flux, such as the former Soviet republics, needed help in policing their respective borders and authorized export-control assistance to numerous countries, including the emerging central European states and Russia.

• In a further demonstration of a joint commitment to nuclear nonproliferation, in March 1996, the governments of the U.S., France, and England agreed to additional provisions to the South Pacific Nuclear Free Zone Treaty, thereby ensuring that this area will be nuclear free. Representatives of the three countries are presently negotiating a comprehensive test ban treaty to end nuclear testing throughout the world— an agreement that is expected to be reached in 1996.

Bosnia

By the time President Clinton was elected, the former Yugoslavia had disintegrated into ethnic battle zones over which three warring factions lay claim: Serbs, Croatians, and Bosnian Muslims. Sarajevo, once a host city to the Winter Olympics, had become a virtual no-man's-land. Reports

President Clinton committed American troops to Bosnia in an effort to prevent further bloodshed in the region and give the new peace accord a chance.

The signing of the Bosnian-Croatian peace agreement on March 18, 1994 allowed civilians free access to Sarajevo for the first time in two years.

of ethnic cleansing, acts of genocide by Serb troops on Bosnia's civilian population, and atrocities being committed by Serbian forces in detention camps shocked the world.

Despite the tragic and nonstop loss of life, the debate over the specific responsibility of the U.S. to end the conflict had raged on for years. While Republicans in Congress strongly favored providing arms to the Bosnian Muslims in order to better defend themselves against the Serbs, President Clinton in turn supported the multinational United Nations peacekeeping force. While the U.N. made some progress—the sustained artillery shelling of Sarajevo's civilian population was temporarily halted, and a War Crimes Tribunal was established—the killing went on.

Relying heavily on the counsel and negotiation skills of special envoy and former State Department official Richard Holbrooke, President Clinton called for a peace summit to be held in Dayton, Ohio, far removed from war-ravaged Bosnia.

Dayton was the first sit-down negotiation session involving representatives from all three rival factions. The tenets of the agreement reached there were memorialized in the Paris Peace Accord signed in December 1995 by all parties to the conflict.

That same month, President Clinton, in the face of virulent opposition, announced one of the most controversial decisions of his tenure as Commander-in-Chief: To commit American troops to Bosnia in an effort to prevent further bloodshed and give the new peace accord a chance. Sending in U.S. troops, the President told the nation in a televised address, would signal other countries that the U.S. was not shirking its responsibilities as the world's most powerful nation. We would not be committing troops to fight a war, he continued, but to ensure lasting peace in Bosnia.

Opposition to such a risky move was understandable, given the dangers involved and the precarious nature of the terrain—Bosnia is considered by many military experts to be among the most geographically perilous regions in Europe. President Clinton went forward with the deployment of 20,000 troops with one proviso: all U.S. forces, while serving as part of the U.N. peacekeeping, would remain under U.S. command at all times.

In Bosnia today, the four-year-long slaughter has ceased. Wanton death and destruction has been replaced by a climate in which Serbs, Muslims, and Croats can stand side by side, if somewhat cautiously, hawking their goods in the town square of the formerly war-torn city of Sarajevo. Children have returned to school, and residents are able to attend their houses of worship, whether it be a church, a synagogue, or a mosque, without fear of being attacked.

Halfway through the one-year U.S.-led North American Treaty Organization (NATO) peacekeeping mission, there are still 18,000 American troops stationed in Bosnia. While relevant questions remain as to how and when to complete an exit without causing a return to war and carnage, Bosnia is scheduled to hold its first free elections in September 1996.

Haiti

For decades, the relationship between the U.S. and Haiti has been mired in controversy. In 1926, President Theodore Roosevelt committed U.S. troops to that Caribbean-island country to quell rioting that threatened the lives of Americans doing business in Port-au-Prince. For 40 years, the local press blamed every regime change on the island on the

CIA. And for two generations, under the leadership of the Duvalier family, the Haitian government, as a matter of policy, both solicited and decried U.S. involvement in its internal affairs.

When the lawfully elected president of Haiti, Reverend Jean Paul Aristide, was ousted by the military and its feared secret police, many Americans thought the U.S., as the most powerful democracy in the hemisphere, should intervene. Typically, others did not, even as boatloads of desperate Haitian refugees sailed for Florida, with some vessels capsizing at sea and losing all aboard.

The President imposed economic sanctions against Haiti after its military rulers refused to restore President Aristide to power. When these sanctions failed to oust the defiant leaders, an invasion of the island was ordered by the White House. But in last-minute negotiations in which the President was represented by former President Jimmy Carter, Senator Sam Nunn, and retired General Colin Powell, the temporary Haitian leader, General Raoul Cédras, agreed to step down, and a peaceful transition of power from the military back to President Aristide was made.

On October 15, 1994, President Aristide was returned to power, and U.S. troops soon returned home. Today, the peace is holding in Haiti. The streets of Port-au-Prince are safer and the flow of illegal refugees to U.S. shores has virtually stopped.

Somalia

The Clinton Administration's ability to deal effectively with Haiti and Bosnia was strengthened by some hard lessons learned in Somalia about the importance for peacekeeping operations to have a clear military mission, firm deadlines, and a defined goal—such as free elections—as part of an exit strategy. When President Clinton took office, the U.S. was already engaged in a humanitarian mission in Somalia on the eastern coast of Africa. Somalian leader Mohammed Farah Aidid had sought international assistance in stopping the famine in his drought-ridden country, and a U.S.-led operation, "Restore Hope," authorized by former President Bush had begun in late 1992.

U.S. troops were pulled out of the humanitarian mission in Somalia after the loss of 18 Army Rangers who were ambushed by a well-armed clan.

In reality, Somalia had no real government. Rather, it served as a private battleground for rival warlords who profited from widespread looting and theft of donated provisions air-dropped to combat famine. In March 1994, five months after the tragic loss of 18 U.S. Army Rangers ambushed by a well-armed clan, President Clinton withdrew all U.S. troops from Somalia without further loss of American lives.

"The U.S. and U.N. peace mission was not an unmitigated success," reported *Foreign Affairs* (May–June 1995), "but it was successful per the original terms of the operation. A human rights disaster was averted, people's lives were saved, and the internal politics of the nation was improved." A year later, while mass starvation in Somalia is no longer a problem, clan fighting continues.

Rwanda

In this tiny, landlocked Central African nation, the horrors of civil war and the mass genocidal murder of hundreds of thousands of innocent

An airlift of $150 million in food and medicine supplies was ordered for Rwanda by the President as he pursued the expansion of U.N. peacekeeping forces in the area.

people, after the death of Rwanda's president in a plane crash in April 1994, appalled the world community. While pursuing the expansion of U.N. peacekeeping forces in the area, the President ordered the immediate airlift of $150 million in relief supplies, including much-needed food and medicine.

The U.S. made it clear to the new leaders of Rwanda, however, that continued international acceptance and assistance, including American recognition, depended upon the establishment of a broad-based government, the rule of law and efforts at national reconciliation. According to *U.S. News and World Report* (April 15, 1996), Rwanda today is "comparatively stable. A new government is making steady progress toward restoring order and infrastructure."

The International Monetary Fund reports that Rwanda's war-ravaged economy grew about 40 percent last year.

The Middle East

If one image could symbolize the Clinton Administration's efforts and commitment in this troubled corner of the world, it would be the famous handshake of peace between Yasser Arafat and Yitzhak Rabin. There, on September 13, 1993, the two leaders celebrated an agreement to remove Israeli troops from Arab towns and cities in the occupied West Bank and to grant self rule by the middle of 1996. To date further negotiations have moved toward granting Palestinians autonomy in return for security guarantees.

Other diplomatic successes include:

• The Israeli-Palestinian Treaty

• The Israeli-Jordan Peace Accord

• The Summit of Peacemakers in Egypt with 29 world and regional leaders to support the Middle East peace process and to counter terrorism

• Securing a written agreement between Israel and Syria to end Hezbollah attacks on Israel and provide security to civilians on both sides of the Lebanon-Israel border.

In addition, the Clinton Administration has had to stay vigilant in dealing with the Middle East's wild card, Saddam Hussein, by dispatching a full reserve of U.S. planes, ships, and ground troops in response to renewed Iraqi military activity at the Kuwaiti border.

Northern Ireland

The Clinton Administration played a critical role in advancing the peace process in Northern Ireland by acknowledging that Sinn Fein, as the political representative of the Irish Republic Army, had a rightful place at the bargaining table to determine the future of Ulster. The President invited Sinn Fein leader Gerry Adams to the White House on St. Patrick's Day in 1995. The U.S. State Department had granted Adams a visa to enter the country for the visit, thereby allowing him to raise support in the U.S. for his cause.

These efforts led directly to the Irish Republican Army announcing a unilateral cease-fire in late 1995. Soon thereafter, President Clinton

visited Northern Ireland. He received an enthusiastic public reception when he promised U.S. support if the Irish renounced violence and participated in the peace process.

President Clinton was represented by former Senator George Mitchell as his personal representative in the negotiations that resulted in a truce between the British Government, the Ulster Defense Association, and the IRA. That cease-fire was broken in April 1996 by renewed IRA bombings in London. Negotiations for a full political solution to the decades-old Northern Ireland standoff will begin in September 1996, with Mitchell representing the United States.

NATO

NATO was established to present a united front in Western Europe to protect that part of the continent against Soviet advance. With the demise of the Soviet Union, the question has been posed whether or not there is any real need for the continued existence of the North American Treaty Organization (NATO). President Clinton has said he not only sees a greater need for NATO given the rapidly changing developments in Central and Eastern Europe, but also an important opportunity to solidify the peace that NATO countries have fought so hard over the years to achieve.

Toward this end, the President, in 1994, led the way in creating NATO's Partnership for Peace, an agreement whereby the current members of the NATO alliance have committed to an orderly process of expansion, admitting new members while modernizing and strengthening the organization. A stronger NATO, it was reasoned, meant the U.S. would never have to go it alone.

For some new "Partner" countries—like Hungary—it was a path to full NATO membership. "For all members," said Anthony Lake, the U.S. National Security Advisor, "it is a powerful incentive to deepen democracy, establish civilian control of the military, and be a responsible member of the global community."

Already, results are positive. In Bosnia, soldiers from more than a dozen "Partner" states have joined with U.S. and NATO troops. And in fact, Hungary, the former Soviet satellite, is the major staging ground for American troops serving in Bosnia.

Cuba

On the afternoon of February 24, 1996, three U.S. civilian aircraft manned by members of a Florida-based Cuban émigré group, Brothers To The Rescue, took off from a Florida airfield and headed for Cuba. One of the aircraft entered Cuban airspace as part of an ongoing operation that previously had dropped anti-Castro leaflets over the streets of Havana. That aircraft eventually turned around and returned safely to Florida. The other two aircraft were not so lucky. Intercepted outside Cuban airspace by a Cuban MIG 29 with permission to attack, the two civilian aircraft were hit by air-to-air heat-seeking missiles and destroyed, killing the four men aboard.

Just 17 days later, with leaders of both political parties putting aside differences and hammering out an acceptable version of a bill that began life as House Resolution 927—also known as the Helms-Burton Bill—President Clinton signed into law the "Cuban Liberty and Democratic Solidarity Act."

The act tightens the existing U.S. embargo on Cuba by imposing additional economic sanctions on the Cuban regime. It also mandates the preparation of a plan for U.S. assistance to a transitional and democratically elected Cuban government, creates a cause of action enabling U.S. nationals to sue those who expropriate or "traffic" in expropriated properties in Cuba, and denies such traffickers entry into the U.S.

"By acting so swiftly," President Clinton said at the signing, "we are sending a powerful message to the Cuban regime that we do not and will not tolerate such conduct."

Five months later, facing mounting pressure from allies—including Canada and France—the President refused to waive the provision of Helms-Burton that allows U.S. citizens to sue foreign firms that are using American assets seized by Cuba over 35 years ago, not long after Fidel Castro came into power. President Clinton did, however, delay filing of

such lawsuits six months. He pledged to use the delay to reach an agreement with allies on a policy toward Cuba.

Land Mine Ban

For decades, countries around the world have faced with horror the devastations that antipersonnel land mines buried long ago during wartime can cause. Children at play, farmers tending their fields, and ordinary travelers are among the victims, with an estimated 25,000 people a year maimed or killed by mines left behind when wars have ended.

In May 1996, President Clinton announced he would seek a worldwide agreement as soon as possible to end the use of all antipersonnel land mines. This follows work already being done by the U.S. to clear mines in 14 nations, from Bosnia to Afghanistan, from Cambodia to Namibia. It also builds on the export moratorium on land mines that the U.S. has observed for four years, and which 32 other nations have joined.

Specifically, the President ordered U.S. Armed Forces to discontinue the use of all so-called "dumb" antipersonnel mines—those which remain active until they are detonated or cleared. The only exception is on the Korean Peninsula, where mines are in place to defend American troops and allies. The rest of these mines in the U.S. arsenal, more than 4 million in all, will be removed from service and destroyed by 1999.

PART TWO

The Inauguration of William Jefferson Clinton at the Capitol on January 20, 1993.

ELECTIVES

It was a bright, cold wintry afternoon in the nation's capital when 46-year-old President-elect William Jefferson Clinton, seated across from President Bush in a matching brown leather armchair, stood on cue, stepped to the podium, and, with his right hand on his grandmother's King James Bible, took the 35-word presidential oath in front of a crowd estimated at 250,000. His election had been a landslide in the electoral college—357 to 168—and he had received 43 percent of the popular vote in a bitter three-way race. Adding the anti-incumbency vote that went to Ross Perot, a whopping 62 percent of the voters voiced their impatience with gridlock. Opting not only for change but for prompt action, voters gave the Democrats control of both the U.S. Senate and House of Representatives as well.

On the very morning that the world's most orderly transfer of power took place in the world's most powerful nation, the *Washington Post* published a list of the 157 campaign promises that had been made by presidential candidate Bill Clinton.

"That a candidate would promise as much as President-elect Clinton did last year might be surprising after one broken campaign pledge—'Read my lips, no new taxes'—caused his predecessor so many problems," wrote the *Post*. "[But] voters wanted detailed answers to their questions. 'Specificity is the character issue of 1992,' George Stephanopoulos, Clinton's communications director, said before last year's New Hampshire primary. This year's character question for

Clinton," the *Post* concluded, "may be keeping his word."

The list of promises printed by the *Post* on Inauguration Day in 1993 serves as the basis for the second part of the presidential report card: Electives. An analysis follows each pledge as well as each group of pledges made on a particular subject, showing to what extent President Clinton has and has not made good on the promises he made during his campaign.

ABORTION

1. Promise: To gain passage of the Freedom of Choice Act, which protects abortion rights and allows some state restrictions, such as parental notification.

Status: Although the President supported passage, it failed to gain enough votes in Congress to become law.

2. Promise: To overturn laws prohibiting federal abortion funding.

Status: During the Reagan and Bush Administrations, these services had been banned by the Hyde Amendment. Now, federal law requires Medicaid to pay for abortions for poor women in cases of rape or incest. ✓ Promise Kept

3. Promise: To repeal Bush Administration rules restricting abortion counseling in clinics that receive federal funds.

Status: In a January 22, 1993, executive memorandum, the President directed that federally funded family planning clinics include abortion as a method of birth control. ✓ Promise Kept

4. Promise: To protect women seeking abortions and health care workers from antiabortion protesters.

Status: The President signed and is enforcing the Freedom of Access to Clinic Law, which provides for the safety of citizens as they enter and exit medical clinics. ✓ Promise Kept

5. Promise: To gain reauthorization of federal family planning programs.

Abortion-rights demonstrators clash with antiabortion demonstrators in front of the Erie Medical Center in Buffalo, New York. President Clinton appears with Kate Michelman, President of the NARAL (National Abortion Rights Action League), at a rally for women's right to choose.

Status: The Administration has increased funding for family planning *Promise Kept* to help women reduce the risk of unintended pregnancies. The funding increase makes family planning information and contraceptives available to millions of women who might not otherwise receive reproductive and other health care services.

6. Promise: To allow testing of the RU-486 abortion pill.

Status: The FDA has fast-tracked RU-486's application for approval, *Promise Kept* and should announce the results of clinical testing by the end of 1996.

SUMMARY:
Promises on Abortion Made—6
Action Taken On—6, or 100%
Achieved Substantial Results—5, or 83%

AGRICULTURE

7. Promise: To open new markets for U.S. products, particularly in Eastern Europe and the former Soviet republics.

Status: The Freedom Support Act, authored by Senator Clayborne Pell (D-Rhode Island) and signed into law by the President, authorized expansion of the Food for Peace program in the former Soviet Union. The Japanese and Korean rice markets and the Japanese and Chinese apple markets were opened up to U.S. producers. With the passage of NAFTA and GATT, international trade barriers have been lowered for all U.S. exports.

✓ Promise
Kept

8. Promise: To expand international food aid programs.

Status: An $800 million Food for Progress program expanded U.S. agricultural exports to Russia. Significant food aid was extended to countries including Angola, Ethiopia, Congo, Croatia, Macedonia, and Mozambique.

✓ Promise
Kept

SUMMARY:
Promises on Agriculture Made—2
Action Taken On—2, or 100%
Achieved Substantial Results—2, or 100%

AIDS

9. Promise: To increase funding for research, treatment, and prevention of HIV/AIDS.

Status: Funding for the Ryan White CARE Act was increased by $231 **Promise Kept** million for outpatient AIDS care for a total of $579 million in fiscal year 1994 (FY94). Further proposals include a 20 percent increase in National Institutes of Health spending for AIDS research. For FY97 the President has proposed an additional $24 million increase in AIDS research and $52 million in supplemental appropriations for programs under the Ryan White CARE Act. The increases will bring treatment to an additional 5,000 to 10,000 HIV and AIDS patients.

10. Promise: To appoint a policy coordinator to enact recommendations of the National Commission on AIDS.

Status: The first federally appointed AIDS czar, Kristine Gebbie, was **Promise Kept** named to focus on consolidating federal resources and address the issues surrounding AIDS.

11. Promise: To speed up federal drug approval process.

Status: The National Task Force on AIDS Drug Development was set **Promise Kept** up as a public/private sector partnership to speed AIDS drugs to the market. The FDA has approved of new labeling indications for six products for HIV and related conditions, and has streamlined its drug approval application process, which will reduce costs and allow new drugs to reach the consumer faster.

12. Promise: To fully fund the Ryan White CARE Act.

Status: The President signed into law the Ryan White CARE Act **Promise Kept** Amendments of 1996 reauthorizing this AIDS program. Under President Clinton, the program's funding has more than doubled since fiscal year 1993.

Police arrest demonstrators in Rockville, Maryland, who are unhappy with the federal government's response to the AIDS crisis.

13. Promise: To launch frank education and prevention programs and support local efforts to distribute condoms in schools.

Status: Community prevention planning was instituted for greater local control over HIV education efforts; the Prevention Marketing Initiative was aimed at young adults to inform them of behaviors that put them at risk for HIV, and included ads promoting both abstinence and consistent use of latex condoms. A memorandum was issued to heads of executive departments and government agencies instructing them to implement ongoing HIV/AIDS education and prevention programs and to develop nondiscriminatory workplace policies for employees with HIV/AIDS. The National AIDS Awareness Advertising Campaign was begun in January 1994.

✓ Promise Kept

14. Promise: To end AIDS-related immigration and travel restrictions.

Status: The White House proposed legislation that was rejected by Congress, resulting in a continuation of this policy.

> **SUMMARY:**
> **Promises on AIDS Made—6**
> **Action Taken On—6, or 100%**
> **Achieved Substantial Results—5, or 83%**

ARMS CONTROL

15. Promise: To gain ratification of START I and START II treaties.

Status: START I entered into force on December 5, 1994. START II
✓ **Promise Kept** was ratified by the Senate in January 1996; the treaty requires Russia and the United States to reduce strategic nuclear arms arsenals by 2/3 from Cold War levels.

16. Promise: To use sanctions to seek stronger export controls from countries with technologies for nuclear and other arms.

Status: Sanctions were placed on China and Pakistan for missile sales,
✓ **Promise Kept** on Thailand for chemical weapons-related exports to Libya, and on Russia for arms sales to Iran. With support and pressure from the White House, a proposal that will allow the President to restrict imports from countries who permit their companies to sell nuclear technologies and equipment to volatile dangerous nations

(e.g., Iran, Iraq, and Libya) is likely to gain Senate approval and become law. A similar provision was proposed by Representative Pete Stark (D-California) in 1991, during the Bush Administration, but it died in the Senate.

17. Promise: To prevent foreign governments from using agricultural and other nonmilitary aid as weapons.

Status: When countries such as Somalia withheld humanitarian U.S. or Red Cross food shipments as a means of ongoing internal suppression, the U.S. government vigorously enforced the prohibition of using nonmilitary aid for military purposes. ✔ **Promise Kept**

18. Promise: To enable the International Atomic Energy Agency (IAEA) to conduct more inspections to stop nuclear proliferation.

Status: Funding for the IAEA has increased $10 million. An agreement was reached with a reluctant North Korea that halts, and will eventually eliminate, its potentially dangerous nuclear weapons program and allows full ongoing IAEA access to North Korea's nuclear sites. At the end of 1995, IAEA inspection agreements were in place with 125 states during which 2,285 inspections had been carried out in 66 states. ✔ **Promise Kept**

19. Promise: To press countries to join the Missile Technology Control Regime (MTCR).

Status: Agreements were concluded with Russia, Ukraine, and China to abide by MTCR guidelines. Hungary and Argentina have joined the MTCR, and Brazil has committed itself publicly to adhere to the MTCR guidelines. ✔ **Promise Kept**

20. Promise: To seek a Comprehensive Test Ban Treaty and an international agreement banning chemical weapons.

Status: The White House sent a global treaty banning toxic weapons ✓**Promise Kept** to the Senate floor in November 1993, where it has been stalled by the GOP majority. President Clinton announced on August 11, 1995, his intentions to push for an international agreement by 1996 that will prohibit nuclear weapons testing. In reaction to the Test Ban Treaty, the United Nations Disarmament conference admitted 23 countries to full membership.

> **SUMMARY:**
> **Promises on Arms Control Made—6**
> **Action Taken On—6, or 100%**
> **Achieved Substantial Results—6, or 100%**

ARTS

21. Promise: To oppose restrictions on grants from the National Endowment for the Arts based on content.

Status: No formal content restrictions on the NEA grants have been ✓**Promise Kept** imposed; however, the "decency standard" may constitute a restriction of sorts.

> **SUMMARY:**
> **Promises on Arts Made—1**
> **Action Taken On—1, or 100%**
> **Achieved Substantial Results—1, or 100%**

BUDGET

22. Promise: To halve the annual federal budget deficit in four years from the $323 billion gap first projected by the Congressional Budget Office for 1993 to $141 billion in 1996.

Status: On August 10, 1993, President Clinton signed into law the largest deficit reduction plan in history. Under the plan, the deficit—as a percentage of GNP, or in actual dollars—has been cut more than 55 percent by 1996. The federal deficit will be the lowest in 15 years according to the latest deficit predictions for the 1996 federal budget. This $117 billion deficit prediction represents a savings of more than $26 billion over the original predictions of the 1993 deficit plan. The deficit will have dropped by more than $700 billion dollars over five years and, for the first time since Harry Truman was president, will have dropped three years in a row.

 Promise Kept

23. Promise: To seek a line-item veto to cut wasteful spending.

Status: President Clinton signed the Republican-sponsored Line-Item Veto Bill, which grants the President the line-item veto in July 1997.

✓ Promise Kept

SUMMARY:
Promises on the Budget Made—2
Action Taken On—2, or 100%
Achieved Substantial Results—2, or 100%

CITIES

24. Promise: To offer tax and regulatory incentives to businesses that create jobs in urban enterprise zones.

Status: The President proposed and signed legislation in August 1993

✓Promise Kept that will award $3.5 billion to 104 empowerment zones and enterprise communities. It was announced in December 1994 which communities will be designated Empowerment Zones in 1995: Six urban communities will each receive $100 million in block grants and business tax breaks, and three rural communities will receive $40 million in assistance and block grants.

25. Promise: To provide funding and block grants to improve infrastructure.

Status: Three hundred million dollars has been appropriated for the

✓Promise Kept new Economic Development Initiative (EDI) of the Fiscal Year 1995 (FY95) budget, which will provide grants to assist financing of economic development projects. The FY96 budget calls for reinventing HUD, which will involve creating new flexible block grants for community economic development and consolidating a number of current formula-based and competitive programs.

26. Promise: To create a network of 100 community development banks to aid low-income entrepreneurs and homeowners.

Status: The President proposed and signed into law the Community

✓Promise Kept Development and Regulatory Improvement Act in August 1994, which authorizes $500 million to encourage a network of new and existing Community Development Banks and Financial

Institutions (CDBFIs) across the country. The Treasury Department projects that the act will lead to approximately $5 billion in new credit for economically distressed communities, provide financial and technical support for as many as 75 new insured community development banks, and support as many as 916 new well-capitalized community development corporations and over 4,000 community development loan funds.

27. Promise: To revise local reinvestment requirements for commercial banks.

Status: The federal banking regulatory agencies are in the process of approving final regulations that will provide clearer and more objective evaluation standards, eliminate unnecessary documentation requirements, and improve the consistency of the Community Reinvestment Act examinations and enforcement efforts. During the Clinton Administration, home-loan approvals for blacks have increased more than 38 percent. The President has threatened to veto any congressional efforts to weaken the act. Promise Kept

28. Promise: To allow cities to spend 15 percent of their federal aid on local priorities.

Status: The Reinventing Government plan would give local governments more flexibility in how they spend their federal aid. Promise Kept

SUMMARY:
   Promises on Cities Made—5
   Action Taken On—5, or 100%
   Achieved Substantial Results—5, or 100%

CIVIL RIGHTS

29. Promise: To oppose racial quotas.

Status: The President ordered a review of the federal government's affir-
✓ Promise Kept mative action programs and concluded that affirmative action
is still an effective tool to expand economic and educational
opportunity. Further, in keeping with the Supreme Court's decision in
Adarand, an affirmative action program may not have quotas, reverse
discrimination, or preferences for unqualified individuals. Nor may programs continue after they have met their stated goals. Thus, during
President Clinton's tenure, racial quotas have been effectively eliminated.

30. Promise: To support and seek passage of an Equal Rights Amendment and federal civil rights laws for homosexuals that exempt religious organizations.

Status: The President testified before the Senate on behalf of legisla-
✓ Promise Kept tion codifying protection of federal civil rights for homosexuals, but legislation did not pass.

31. Promise: To raise caps on damages in workplace discrimination cases.

Status: The President endorsed House and Senate bills in the 103rd
Congress, which did not pass.

SUMMARY:
Promises on Civil Rights Made—3
Action Taken On—3, or 100%
Achieved Substantial Results—2, or 67%

CRIME AND DRUGS

32. Promise: To put 100,000 new police officers to work and expand community policing.

Status: The President proposed and signed the Crime Bill, which will put 100,000 new police officers on the street. To date, more than 1,200 communities have already received grants to hire 60,000 police. In FY95, $1.3 billion was appropriated for cities to hire new police if they agreed to establish a community policing plan. ✓ **Promise Kept**

33. Promise: To create a National Police Corps to put military personnel and unemployed veterans to work in law enforcement.

Status: The Crime Bill created a Police Corps to give young people money for college and train them in community policing. A total of $100 million has been authorized for the Police Corps program and $100 million has been authorized for in-service law enforcement scholarships. ✓ **Promise Kept**

34. Promise: To have first-time, nonviolent offenders serve out their sentences in community boot camps.

Status: The Crime Bill includes a grant program for state correction agencies to build correctional facilities, including boot camps, to ensure that additional space will be available to put—and keep—violent offenders. ✓ **Promise Kept**

35. Promise: To enact tough penalties for assaults against women and children to deter domestic violence.

Status: The Crime Bill includes formula and competitive grant programs which support police and prosecutor efforts to strengthen ✓**Promise Kept** enforcement and provide services to victims in such cases. It authorized $325 million for battered women's shelters and other domestic violence prevention activities. A national 24-hour Domestic Violence Hotline was established: 1-800-799-SAFE. The Crime Bill also provides for the prohibition of firearms sales to persons who have received family violence restraining orders, and has enhanced penalties for interstate domestic violence.

36. Promises: To increase federal funding for school-based and community drug education programs and treatment clinics.

Status: The Crime Bill authorizes funding for the President's Prevention Council, rural anticrime and drug efforts, and a ✓**Promise Kept** local Crime Prevention Block Grant program to be distributed to local governments, including a "Zero Tolerance" gun policy in schools.

37. Promise: To provide federal matching funds for crime prevention in crime-ridden communities.

Status: Up to 15 cities will be elected for model crime prevention programs targeted at high-crime neighborhoods. ✓**Promise Kept**

38. Promise: To impose a five-day waiting period on handgun purchases, ban assault weapons with no legitimate hunting purpose, and limit access to multiple-round clips.

Status: Under the Brady Bill which was signed into law on November 30, 1993, there is a five-day waiting period on handgun purchases. The manufacture of 19 military-style assault weapons, ✓**Promise Kept** assault weapons with specific combat features, "copycat" models, and certain high-capacity ammunition magazines of more than 10 rounds were banned as part of the Crime Bill.

39. Promise: To seek jail terms for serious white-collar criminals in "real" prisons, not high-tech "summer camps."

Status: The Crime Bill prohibits favoritism for white-collar criminals when making prison assignments. ✓ Promise Kept

40. Promise: To crack down on hate crimes.

Status: The Crime Bill includes tougher penalties for federal hate crimes. Hate crime violators will now be sentenced to an additional 12–15 months in prison. ✓ Promise Kept

SUMMARY:
Promises on Crime and Drugs Made—9
Action Taken On—9, or 100%
Achieved Substantial Results—9, or 100%

DEFENSE

41. Promise: To save $100 billion in defense spending over five years, or $60 billion more than the Bush Administration proposed.

Status: The $1.241 trillion military spending plan for FY94-98 matched this pledge, as measured against the revised $1.365 trillion Bush defense budget for the same years. ✓ Promise Kept

42. Promise: To cut military personnel by offering voluntary early retirement and prorated pensions for those who have served 15–20 years.

Status: Benefits were offered to certain military personnel classes to

✓ Promise Kept — cut levels.

43. Promise: To pay retiring personnel for a year of retraining.

Status: Several retraining programs have been implemented since

✓ Promise Kept — January 1993.

44. Promise: To build a fleet of C-17 cargo planes to expand sea and airlift capabilities and enhance rapid-deployment forces.

Status: On June 3, 1996, the Air Force contracted with McDonnell

✓ Promise Kept — Douglas and Pratt & Whitney for the construction and sale of 80 C-17 Globemaster III transports. With the delivery of these 80 planes, the Air Force's C-17 fleet will increase to 120 by the year 2004.

45. Promise: To reduce U.S. forces in Europe to 75,000–100,000 troops, but maintain commitment to NATO.

Status: A reduction of troops has been made close to the promised

✓ Promise Kept — 100,000 level. The White House proposed and won Allied approval for NATO's gradual expansion to Europe's new democracies. The U.S. led the way for NATO and Central Eastern European (CEE) countries to set up the "Partnership for Peace" (PFP), offering former Soviet republics and CEE nations practical military ties with NATO. The first PFP military exercise was held in Poland in September 1996.

46. Promise: To maintain U.S. military presence in Korea.

Status: The Korean theater currently holds 37,000 American troops. Patriot missiles were sent in 1994 when a crisis loomed in the area.

✔ Promise Kept

47. Promise: To maintain 10 carrier battle groups instead of 12.

Status: As a result of bottom-up review of the military, it was decided that 11 carriers were required even though the White House fought for 10.

48. Promise: To develop short- and medium-range missile defenses and continue research on limited long-range missile defenses.

Status: The White House requested over $2 billion in FY95 funds to continue research on national military defense and to develop highly effective theater missile defenses.

✔ Promise Kept

49. Promise: To cut spending on large, space-based missile defenses.

Status: Funding has been reduced for space-based lasers and missiles. First, budget cuts were made in the Strategic Defense Initiative Office (SIDO, or Star Wars) by 40 percent over the Bush FY94 budget, which saved $2.5 billion. Then, SIDO was eliminated and replaced with the creation of the Ballistic Missile Defense Organizations.

✔ Promise Kept

50. Promise: To reverse the ban on homosexuals in the military.

Status: A new, more tolerant policy took effect February 28, 1994, commonly referred to as "don't ask, don't tell."

✓ **Promise Kept**

SUMMARY:
Promises on Defense Made—10
Action Taken On—10, or 100%
Achieved Substantial Results—9, or 90%

ECONOMY AND JOBS

51. Promise: To create a National Economic Council.

Status: Executive Order 12835 established the NEC on January 25, 1993.

✓ **Promise Kept**

52. Promise: To end tax incentives that encourage companies to export plants and jobs.

Status: President Clinton's 1993 Economic Plan added a provision in the Internal Revenue Code that imposes a current tax on U.S. shareholders of foreign corporations who transfer profits and working capital to passive interests abroad. By reducing the opportunities for unlimited deferral, the incentive to shift plants overseas is significantly reduced. Also, transfer pricing initiatives have reduced the opportunity to shift income to foreign tax havens.

✓ **Promise Kept**

53. Promise: To provide investment tax credits to companies that invest in U.S.-based plants and American-made equipment.

Status: An incremental investment tax credit was proposed in 1993, but did not pass in Congress.

54. Promise: To make foreign companies with businesses in the United States pay the same taxes as U.S. companies.

Status: In July 1994, the Treasury Department issued final regulations governing transfer pricing. These rules, backed by severe penalties, are expected to ensure that an accurate amount of multinational company profits are subject to tax in the U.S. In addition, the 1993 Economic Plan included a provision that will make it more ✔ **Promise Kept** difficult for multinational companies to strip earnings out of the U.S. through deductible payments, such as interest.

55. Promise: To offer a 50 percent tax exclusion to those who make long-term investments in new businesses.

Status: As part of its 1993 Economic Plan, the Administration enacted a 50 percent capital-gains tax exclusion targeted at investments in small businesses. The provision allows investors who buy newly issued stock in small businesses and hold that stock for more than five years to receive a 50 percent cut in the capital-gains tax on the profit from the sale of the stock. The President also supports the Hatch-Lieberman bill, which would allow the profit from long-term investments in small business stock to be excluded from capital-gains tax. The percentage of profit that would be excluded would increase from the current 50 percent exclusion to a 75 percent exclusion. And if the profits are reinvested in another qualified small business stock, the tax would be 100 per- ✔ **Promise Kept** cent deferred.

56. Promise: To create a $20-billion-a-year fund for spending on transportation and roads, communications and information networks, and environmental technology.

Status: A five-year $20 billion Defense Reinvestment initiative was **✓Promise Kept** announced in March 1993 that is centered on four major areas of new investment: (1) worker training and adjustment; (2) community reinvestment; (3) "dual-use" technologies with both commercial and military applications; and (4) new civilian technology investments that provide diversification opportunities. The EPA's enacted budget for environmental technology doubled over the FY93–FY95 period to $139 million. The President proposed that $1.3 billion be spent to develop corridors outside of the Northeast for the next generation of High Speed Rail which is intended to relieve air and intercity travel congestion. Further it has been asserted that High Speed Rail will reduce America's petroleum dependence. Other new funding for private sector technology partnerships includes: (1) the U.S. Climate Change Action Program—$232 million FY95 enacted, and (2) Partnership for a New Generation of Vehicles (Clean Car)—$269 million FY95 enacted. The President's FY96 budget proposes establishing a network of state Infrastructure Banks that will allow states to leverage federal funding, thereby achieving a greater level of investment from a given level of federal resources.

57. Promise: To make business tax credits for research and development permanent.

Status: The Administration secured a three-year extension of the **✓Promise Kept** Research and Development tax credit, retroactive to June 30, 1992, and effective through June 20, 1995. Although the President is committed to the tax credit, he vetoed a provision to continue it beyond mid-1995 because the GOP attached it to a budget proposal he found unacceptable.

58. Promise: To develop new commercial technologies through a new civilian research and development agency.

Status: Defense R&D has been refocused on "dual-uses" (commercial-military) technologies. To reflect the new commercial focus, the word Defense was removed from DARPA's name (Defense Advanced Research Projects Agency). The largest multiagency technology program ever, the Technology Reinvestment Project, was launched to stimulate dual-uses technology. Funding for the Advanced Technology Program has increased from $68 million in FY93 to $450 million in FY95. The National Science and Technology Council was created to help define and achieve science and technology goals. Government/industry partnerships have been launched in critical technologies such as flat-panel displays, the "Clean Car," semiconductors and environmental technologies necessary for sustainable economic development. The Administration has been outspoken against congressional cuts to science research and development programs. ✓ Promise Kept

59. Promise: To raise the minimum wage to keep pace with inflation.

Status: In 1996, President Clinton repeatedly called on Congress to raise the minimum wage; in July, legislation was finally passed. ✓ Promise Kept

60. Promise: To limit deductions for executive pay.

Status: As part of his Economic Plan, President Clinton signed legislation that denies a deduction to any publicly held corporation for compensation exceeding $1 million paid to CEOs or certain other high-ranking officers. Some forms of compensation, including quali-

✔ Promise Kept fied retirement plan contributions and performance-based awards approved by shareholders, are exempt from the cap.

61. Promise: To allow businesses to deduct bonus and severance packages for executives only if other employees are offered similar packages.

Status: No action taken.

SUMMARY:
Promises on Economy and Jobs Made—11
Action Taken On—10, or 91%
Achieved Substantial Results—9, or 82%

EDUCATION

62. Promise: To create a national service program that allows college students to repay federal loans with community work.

Status: President Clinton proposed and signed the National and

✔ Promise Kept Community Service Trust Act creating AmeriCorps on September 21, 1993. AmeriCorps gives young people the chance to spend a year or more helping their communities while earning an award of $4,725 per year of service to pay for college or job training. Twenty thousand Americans have become AmeriCorps members in its first year, which is more than the Peace Corps at its height.

63. Promise: To fully fund Head Start and other programs recommended by the National Commission on Children.

Status: Funding for Head Start has been increased by $800 million over two years. ✓ **Promise Kept**

64. Promise: To enact national standards for public schools to be measured with examinations on core subjects.

Status: The President proposed and signed the Goals 2000: Educate America Act, which codifies national education goals and supports state reform efforts, including state standards. To date, 48 states are currently participating in the program. ✓ **Promise Kept**

65. Promise: To help students not going to college develop job skills through a national apprenticeship program.

Status: The School-to-Work Opportunities Act was signed on May 4, 1994, to provide $250 million in 1995 for all 50 states to plan and develop their own diverse school-to-work initiatives. ✓ **Promise Kept**

66. Promise: To require employers to spend 1.5 percent of payroll costs on education and training for all workers.

Status: Government funding for reemployment services has been increased by 150 percent, enabling 400,000 more workers to participate in retraining in 1995 than in 1993.

67. Promise: To encourage competition in education by giving parents public school choice.

Status: Charter School legislation was passed which encourages state and local decision making to set up public school choice. ✓ **Promise Kept**

68. Promise: To increase Chapter One funding to "level the playing field" for disadvantaged students.

Status: An additional $500 million was requested for FY95, bringing the total budget of Chapter One to $7.2 billion.

✔ Promise Kept

69. Promise: To give school systems flexibility to use federal funds to reduce class sizes or as they see fit.

Status: The establishment of Goals 2000 and the reauthorization of the Elementary and Secondary Schools Act provides flexibility of disbursement of federal funds with full accountability for the desired results.

✔ Promise Kept

70. Promise: To develop programs that help disadvantaged parents work with their children on school assignments.

Status: The Elementary and Secondary Education Act reauthorization promotes partnerships between schools and families. The Family Support and Family Preservation Act authorizes $1 billion to support programs that help parents teach their children.

✔ Promise Kept

71. Promise: To provide funds for security and metal detectors at schools that need them.

Status: The President proposed and signed the Safe and Drug Free Schools and Community Act and Safe Schools Act, which provided $480 million in FY95 to help schools fight violence and drug abuse. Schools may use the funds for activities such as conflict resolution, after-school programs, and drug prevention programs. Schools may use up to 25 percent of their funds to purchase metal detectors, develop safe school zones, and hire school security personnel.

✔ Promise Kept

72. Promise: To require large federal contractors to sponsor jobs and after-school employment for disadvantaged youths.

Status: No action taken.

73. Promise: To promote bilingual education programs in which students learn core subjects in their native languages while also studying English.

Status: In FY96, President Clinton requested that $300 million be funded to the federal office for Bilingual Education. ✓ Promise Kept

> **SUMMARY:**
> **Promises on Education Made—12**
> **Action Taken On—11, or 90%**
> **Achieved Substantial Results—10, or 85%**

ELECTIONS AND GOVERNMENT

74. Promise: To support District of Columbia statehood.

Status: Prior to the House vote, which denied the measure to make Washington, D.C., the 51st state, President Clinton sent a letter to Capitol Hill in which he argued, "It is fundamentally unfair that residents of the District are denied full representation and participation in our national life." To further persuade the House he sent some aides to lobby for the measure. ✓ Promise Kept

75. Promise: To voluntarily cap spending in congressional races and reduce contributions from Political Action Committees from $5,000 to the $1,000 limit on individuals.

Status: The White House supported a comprehensive campaign finance reform bill in the 103rd Congress, but it was killed by filibuster in the Senate.

76. Promise: To end unlimited "soft money" contributions to parties.

Status: The White House supported the campaign finance reform bill in the 103rd Congress, but it was killed by filibuster in the Senate.

77. Promise: To restrict prices on TV ad time for candidates.

Status: The White House supported the campaign finance reform bill in the 103rd Congress, but it was killed by filibuster in the Senate.

78. Promise: To sign the "Motor Voter Act."

Status: The President proposed and signed the National Voter ✓ **Promise Kept** Registration Act on May 20, 1993. The Motor Voter law makes it easier for 70 million unregistered Americans to vote by allowing them to register when they get their driver's licenses. Already 11 million Americans have registered under the new program, the greatest expansion of the voter registration rolls since the 19th century.

79. Promise: To require lobbyists to disclose contributions to members of a congressional committee before they can testify.

Status: On January 1, 1996, a new lobbying reform law went into effect. The law broadens the definition of who is a lobbyist and requires that lobbyists register and disclose their activities. The law represents the first significant change since the 1946 law that first required lobbyists to register. ✓ **Promise Kept**

80. Promise: To end tax breaks for lobbying expenses.

Status: President Clinton's 1993 Economic Plan repealed the tax provision, which dated back to 1962, that allowed businesses to deduct the cost of their lobbying expenses. ✓ **Promise Kept**

81. Promise: To make top appointees pledge not to lobby agencies within their jurisdiction for five years after leaving office.

Status: Executive Order 12834 entitled "Ethics Commitments by Executive Branch Appointees" was signed on January 20, 1993, restricting all senior appointees in executive agencies from lobbying agencies within their jurisdiction for five years after leaving office. ✓ **Promise Kept**

82. Promise: To reduce the White House staff by 25 percent and cut 100,000 federal jobs through attrition.

Status: By September 1994, 350 White House jobs had been cut from a staff of 1,394 during the Bush Administration—a 25 percent reduction. Federal employment has already been reduced by 100,000 positions. Under the recommendations of the National Performance Review, the federal payroll will be cut by 272,000. During this, the fourth year of President Clinton's first term, the size of government is the smallest pro rata since Franklin Roosevelt took office. ✓ **Promise Kept**

83. Promise: To cut 3 percent in agency administrative costs.

Status: Executive Order 12837, signed in February 1993, requires that

✓**Promise** the federal government reduce its administrative expenses
Kept 14 percent by FY97. Already, administrative costs reductions
have exceeded 3 percent.

84. Promise: To appoint more women and minorities to government jobs.

Status: The President has appointed the most diverse cabinet and

✓**Promise** Administration in history, with six women, four African-
Kept Americans, and two Hispanics in the cabinet. Nearly half
of all appointees are women (44 percent). Through the end of
August 1994, 59 percent of President Clinton's judicial nominees to
both the federal district court and the federal court of appeals were
women or minorities. This is compared with 14 percent and 24
percent for female and minority appointments made during the
Reagan and Bush Administrations, respectively. The President's
record surpasses even that of President Jimmy Carter who, with 34
percent, is credited as the first President to stress diversity on the
federal bench.

SUMMARY:
Promises Made on Elections and Government—11
Action Taken On—11, or 100%
Achieved Substantial Results—8, or 64%

ENERGY AND THE ENVIRONMENT

85. Promise: To oppose increasing federal excise gas taxes or increased reliance on nuclear power.

Status: No new nuclear power plants have been constructed on U.S. soil in the past four years. The President signed a $0.043 per gallon tax increase on transportation fuels. ✓ Partially Kept

86. Promise: To raise Corporate Average Fuel Economy (CAFE) standards for automakers from 27.5 miles per gallon to between 40 and 45.

Status: For the 1996 and 1997 model years, light truck fuel economy standards were increased from 20.6 to 20.7 miles per gallon. CAFE standards remain set at 27.5 miles per gallon.

87. Promise: To convert federal vehicle fleet to natural gas.

Status: An Executive Order increased the number of federal vehicles that should use alternative fuels to 11,000 in 1994. The Clean Cities program ensures the Executive Order levels will be exceeded. ✓ Promise Kept

88. Promise: To encourage renewable and alternative energy projects with tax incentives.

Status: Federal partnerships have been launched to cost-share renewable energy deployment. The renewable energy budget was increased 20 percent and an investment tax credit of 10 percent was made permanent for investments in alternative energy projects. ✓ Promise Kept

89. Promise: To use highway spending to encourage car pools and mass transit.

Status: While cutting the budget, President Clinton has managed to invest more in transit than any President in history. Mass transit

spending alone has increased 21 percent from 1993 to 1995. The EPA has worked with business and state and local governments on pro-grams to encourage experimentation in transportation.

✓ Promise Kept

90. Promise: To change regulations and building standards to make energy efficiency profitable for utilities and consumers.

Status: The President is working to change EPA rules and procedures to reduce paperwork requirements for businesses by 10 million hours and allowing businesses to write their own rules if they can do it cleaner and cheaper.

✓ Promise Kept

91. Promise: To curb industrial and toxic emissions and expand markets for recycled products with tax incentives.

Status: An Executive Order was signed requiring a 50 percent reduction of toxic emissions from federal facilities by 1999. The President issued a second Executive Order requiring that all federal purchases of recycled products such as printing and writing contain 20 percent postconsumer material by the end of 1999.

✓ Promise Kept

92. Promise: To enforce environmental laws with jail terms for corporate polluters when necessary.

Status: Over 200 criminal environmental cases were referred by the EPA to the Department of Justice in FY94. Criminal charges were brought against 250 individual and corporate defen-dants with 99 years of jail sentences and $36.8 million in criminal fines assessed that year. In fall of 1995, the EPA was forced to raise the stan-dards of cases that it will prosecute to "significant and egregious cases" because of scarce resources.

✓ Promise Kept

93. Promise: To push utilities to consider the social and economic costs of fuel sources with incentives to adopt least-cost planning.

Status: The President's 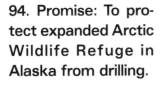 Climate Change Action plan launched a program to advocate integrated resource planning and expanded technical and financial assistance to utilities, as well as state regulation to implement reforms. Over 800 electric utilities comprising 80 percent of all the electricity generated in the U.S. are signing agreements with the Department of Energy to voluntarily reduce consumers' energy use.

This logging road cuts across a clear-cut area of the Alagash region of Maine, demonstrating the seriousness of environmental degradation in the United States.

94. Promise: To protect expanded Arctic Wildlife Refuge in Alaska from drilling.

Status: The President vetoed a bill that would have opened the Arctic National Wildlife Refuge to oil and gas drilling.

95. Promise: To require companies to recover some of the waste they generate or buy "credits" from companies that do.

Status: The Clinton Administration's Hazardous Waste Identification Rule is the EPA's first nationwide attempt to consider site-specific conditions when regulating waste management. The proposed rule provides strong incentives for waste minimization and pollution prevention. Further it should free up $80 million in industry savings, which could then be used to devise solutions for high-risk waste management.

Promise Kept

96. Promise: To pass the Clean Water Act, which includes incentives to reduce "non-point-source" pollution from household chemicals, pesticides, and other substances.

Status: The White House proposed a comprehensive set of Clean Water Act reforms, but Congress failed to act. Congress has attempted to pass a new significantly weakened Clean Water Act, however the President has repeatedly stated that he will use the veto to protect the environment and the Clean Water Act's programs and standards.

97. Promise: To allow citizens to sue federal agencies for ignoring environmental laws and regulations.

Status: The Clean Water Act reauthorization proposal supported the rights of citizens to sue the federal government. In addition, the Administration has aggressively implemented the Federal Facilities Compliance Act, which provides citizens with the right to sue the federal government for violation of the nation's solid and hazardous waste laws.

Promise Kept

98. Promise: To stick to "no net loss" wetlands policy.

Status: The White House introduced the Wetlands Plan to preserve the nation's wetlands. Over $1.5 billion were committed over seven years to help restore the Florida Everglades. The Clinton Administration fought a Senate wetlands reform bill that would have reduced the amount of land under federal enforcement by 75 percent and created exemptions for special interests and activities. Further, the bill would hinder state wetland conservation efforts. To date the bill has been stalled in the Senate. ✓ Promise Kept

99. Promise: To limit carbon dioxide emissions to 1990 levels by 2000.

Status: A plan to limit carbon dioxide emissions to 1990 levels in the year 2000 has been issued, already resulting in a reduction in toxic pollutions from chemical plants by 90 percent and dangerous incinerator emissions by 98 percent. ✓ Promise Kept

100. Promise: To push major banks to reduce debt burdens on developing nations in exchange for land conservation efforts.

Status: No action taken.

SUMMARY:
Promises on Energy and the Environment Made—16
Action Taken On—13.5, or 84%
Achieved Substantial Results—12.5, or 78%

FAMILY PLANNING

101. Promise: To allow U.S. funds to support international family planning and population control efforts.

Status: The Mexico City Policy which banned funding to worldwide family planning groups was revoked by Presidential ✔*Promise Kept* Memorandum on January 22, 1993. Roughly $40 million—the first funding since 1985—was in the budget for FY94. In FY95, the enacted amount was $50 million. The Administration announced that by the year 2000 comprehensive family planning services would be available to "every woman in the world who wants them."

> **SUMMARY:**
> **Promises on Family Planning Made—1**
> **Action Taken On—1, or 100%**
> **Achieved Substantial Results—1, or 100%**

FAMILIES

102. Promise: To pass a Family and Medical Leave Act giving workers 12 weeks of unpaid time off a year to care for newborn children or sick relatives.

Status: Though President Bush vetoed Family and Medical Leave leg-✔*Promise Kept* islation twice, President Clinton signed this legislation into law on February 5, 1993, which offers employees 12 weeks of unpaid, job-guaranteed leave for childbirth, adoption, or personal or family illness. More than 40 million American workers are covered under this legislation.

103. Promise: To crack down on parents who avoid child support.

Status: The Administration has a strong child support enforcement program. The program provides for the suspension of the deadbeat parent's driver's license, encourages states to adopt statewide new-hire reporting programs, and tracks delinquent parents across state lines. In its first national push to crack down on deadbeat parents, the Department of Justice filed 28 cases seeking over $1 million in overdue payments in December 1994, and more than 200 cases are under review. Also, each of the 94 U.S. attorneys has designated a child support enforcement coordinator, and prosecution guidelines have been developed to assist them in going after the most egregious violators. President Clinton's Work and Responsibility Act, introduced in June 1994, includes the toughest child support provisions ever. These provisions would double child support collections to $20 billion by 2000 and place more emphasis on the responsibility of fathers and the withholding of wages of those who do not regularly pay their child support. ✔ Promise Kept

104. Promise: To create a child care network like the network of public schools and enforce new standards on child care facilities.

Status: Every budget submitted by President Clinton has included increases in funding to improve child care and expand child care services. The first ever National Childcare Information Center was launched to help share promising practices across state lines. ✔ Promise Kept

> **SUMMARY:**
> **Promises on Families Made—3**
> **Action Taken On—3, or 100%**
> **Achieved Substantial Results—3, or 100%**

HEALTH CARE

105. Promise: To provide coverage to all Americans with cost controls by requiring employers to buy private insurance or pay into a public system.

Status: The President's Health Care Security Act (HSA) was killed in Congress. The Kassebaum-Kennedy Bill (S. 1028), which the President supports, addresses the issue of affordability, recommending the implementation of cost controls. The bill also prohibits insurance companies from denying coverage to workers when they change jobs, and helps maintain coverage for those who lose their jobs. Furthermore, it prohibits them from denying coverage to employers.

106. Promise: To allow people to choose services from competing local networks of insurers, hospitals, clinics, and doctors, who will be paid a fixed rate.

Status: Included in the Health Care Security Act, killed in Congress.

107. Promise: To provide a core benefits package that includes ambulatory physician and inpatient hospital care, prescription drugs, basic mental health coverage, and expanded access to preventative treatments and routine screening.

Status: Included in the Health Care Security Act, killed in Congress.

108. Promise: To create a board of consumers, providers, and representatives from government, business, and labor to

establish a core package of benefits and annual health budget targets.

Status: Included in the Health Care Security Act, killed in Congress. In an attempt to further the goals of the original board called for under the Health Care Security Act, the President has established several boards to improve health care quality. These are the Foundation for Accountability, the Medicare Managed Care Quality Improvement Program, and the Medicare/Medicaid Health Plan Employer Data and Information. ✓ Promise Kept

109. Promise: To require insurers to cover individuals with any preexisting conditions, charge all businesses in a community the same rate, and streamline billing practices to cut administrative costs.

Status: Included in the Health Care Security Act, killed in Congress. A focal point of the Kassebaum-Kennedy Bill (S. 1028), exclusions for preexisting conditions would be limited. ✓ Partially Kept

110. Promise: To phase in requirements for small employers until costs are reduced.

Status: Included in the Health Care Security Act, killed in Congress. ✓ Promise Kept

111. Promise: To allow small employers to pool to receive more favorable rates from insurers.

Status: Included in the Health Care Security Act, killed in Congress. The Kassebaum-Kennedy Bill (S. 1028) increases the availability of health insurance for small businesses. The ✓ Promise Kept

President's Balanced Budget proposal for FY96 makes it easier for small businesses to buy and maintain affordable health insurance through the use of voluntary purchasing cooperatives.

112. Promise: To eliminate tax breaks for prescription drug manufacturers whose prices increase faster than incomes.

Status: President Clinton proposed and signed legislation, as part of his 1993 Economic Plan, that seeks to eliminate drug price gouging. Subsequently, 17 pharmaceutical industry executives, representing two-thirds of the U.S. pharmaceutical market, agreed to hold price increases at or below the general inflation rate.

✓ Promise Kept

113. Promise: To expand Medicare benefits for the elderly and disabled to include more options for long-term care.

Status: Included in the Health Care Security Act, killed in Congress. The Administration's Balanced Budget Plan protects Medicare from the 104th Congress's attempts to cut it.

✓ Partially Kept

SUMMARY:
Promises on Health Care Made—9
Action Taken On—9, or 100%
Achieved Substantial Results—5, or 55%

HOUSING

114. Promise: To hold a Housing and Homelessness Summit with urban leaders to develop poverty and housing programs.

Status: HUD Secretary Henry Cisneros held 18 interactive homeless forums in as many cities and, with the Vice President, hosted a National Housing and Community Development Conference attended by over 2,000 people. These forums led to the publication of the Federal Plan to End Homelessness. ✔ **Promise Kept**

115. Promise: To transfer 10 percent of all federal housing to churches and other nonprofit community groups for the homeless.

Status: The Administration supports the McKinney program which provides nonprofit homeless organizations the opportunity to have first bid at all surplus federal property. Legislation has been proposed to give local nonprofit organizations a direct role in determining the use of HUD homeless resources. ✔ **Promise Kept**

116. Promise: To use housing at closed military bases for the homeless.

Status: The Administration is backing new procedures to balance the needs of the homeless population with those of the communities in which closed military bases exist. In place at Lowry AFB, Long Beach, California, and elsewhere. ✔ **Promise Kept**

117. Promise: To provide federal support to programs that restore old housing to sell to low-income home buyers.

Status: This support is included in the Housing and Community Development Act of 1993. The Administration is launching an innovative public-private partnership program which encourages pension funds to invest in the production and rehabilitation of affordable multifamily housing. This initiative ✔ **Promise Kept**

will create 3,500 units of affordable housing for working families and the elderly.

118. Promise: To attract investment with a permanent low-income housing tax credit.

Status: The President extended the low-income housing tax credit, which spurred the private development of low-income housing and helped to build more than 120,000 homes each year.

✓ Promise Kept

119. Promise: To provide increased federal funding for maintenance of existing public housing.

Status: The budget increased from $3.2 billion in FY94 to $3.7 billion in FY95.

✓ Promise Kept

120. Promise: To raise the ceiling on Federal Housing Authority mortgage insurance to 95 percent of the price of a home in typical metropolitan areas.

Status: Legislation to raise the ceiling was introduced in the 103rd Congress and passed in the House, but failed in Senate.

✓ Promise Kept

121. Promise: To expand local authority to make more low-income rental units available through the HOME Program.

Status: In FY94 and FY95, about 19,000 families were funded with rental assistance through the HOME program. HOME is funded at $2 billion for FY95. Proposed full funding of HOME in FY95 and reduced regulatory impediments to local use.

✓ Promise Kept

SUMMARY:
Promises on Housing Made—8
Action Taken On—8, or 100%
Achieved Substantial Results—8, or 100%

IMMIGRATION

122. Promise: To give temporary asylum to political refugees from Haiti until that country's government is restored.

Status: U.S. sanctions were applied until the democratically elected Haitian President Aristide was restored to power.

✓ Promise Kept

123. Promise: To cut the two-year waiting period for people seeking visas to the United States who are separated from immediate family members, and reduce the backlog of extended family members in similar situations.

Status: No action taken.

124. Promise: To close sweatshops and "abusive farm labor contractors" that rely on illegal immigration.

Status: President Clinton fought an amendment to the House Immigration Bill which would grant up to 250,000 temporary work visas to foreign farmworkers. The Immigration Bill provides for tighter immigration restrictions, including increased border patrol. Proponents of the amendment argued that the visas are necessary because of the 1.6 million seasonal workers needed to harvest America's crops, some 800,000 are illegal. The President opposed the amendment because it would increase illegal immigration, take

jobs from American citizens, and lower wages and work standards for American workers. The Immigration and Naturalization Services has strengthened enforcement of employer sanction laws to deter hiring of illegal immigrants. Under the Clinton Administration, 51,600 illegal and criminal aliens were deported in 1995, a 15 percent increase over 1994.

✓ Promise Kept

125. Promise: To use trade agreements with Latin American neighbors to raise wages in that region, discourage immigration, and protect U.S. jobs.

Status: The passage of the North America Free Trade Agreement (NAFTA) and the Uruguay Round of GATT helps to provide better-paying jobs and create more stability in the surrounding Latin American regions.

✓ Promise Kept

SUMMARY:
Promises on Immigration Made—4
Action Taken On—3, or 75%
Achieved Substantial Results—3, or 75%

INTERNATIONAL RELATIONS

126. Promise: To link most-favored-nation trading status for China with progress on human rights and nuclear proliferation.

Status: Most-favored-nation status was linked to China's human rights record for one year. Although the Administration claims not to be satisfied with China's progress in the area of human rights, it delivered MFN in favor of increased dialogue and rule-of-law programs, and continued Tiananmen Square sanctions, a ban on munitions imports from China, and vigorous enforcement of U.S. laws on prison labor exports. ✓ **Promise Kept**

127. Promise: To seek U.N. authorization for air strikes against forces that disrupt relief efforts in Bosnia while using U.S. and European naval forces to tighten economic sanctions against Serbia and Montenegro.

Status: The U.S. is participating in a NATO force to uphold the Paris Peace Agreement. The U.N. force will maintain the peace and the United States forces will remain present to ensure that the region returns to a state of normalcy and stability. ✓ **Promise Kept**

128. Promise: To end reported atrocities in Serbian detention camps with international military force if necessary, and punish those responsible for atrocities in Bosnia under international law.

Status: The U.N. War Crimes Tribunal is presently investigating mass grave sites, and is looking to prosecute the leaders responsible for the atrocities. Mr. Karadzic and General Ratko Muratovic were indicted by the Tribunal; their apprehension and prosecution, however, is unlikely because of the political climate in the republic. ✓ **Promise Kept**

129. Promise: To get full accounting of POWs and MIAs before normalizing relations with Vietnam.

Status: The Hanoi government has been very helpful in uncovering 200 documents giving the location of ✓ **Promise Kept**

American servicemen killed during the Vietnam War. The move to recognize Vietnam is supported by American business and Senator John McCain (R-Arizona), a former POW.

130. Promise: To increase political and economic pressure on Haiti's current leadership to restore that country's democratically elected government.

Status: Democracy was restored to Haiti on October 15, 1994, by a U.S.-led multinational coalition force that peacefully returned President Aristide and his constitutionally established government to power.

Promise Kept

131. Promise: To encourage more private investment in the former Soviet Union.

Status: Secretary of Commerce Ron Brown led the Administration's efforts to U.S. business interests around the world, and was in fact killed in a plane crash on just such a mission. An investment treaty with Moldova was transmitted to the Senate, which provided the basis for dispute resolution and legal agreements that are necessary to form the framework for economic investment in the countries of the former Soviet Union.

Promise Kept

132. Promise: To guarantee loans for Israel to help settle Soviet Jews.

Status: The loan guarantees remain in place.

Promise Kept

133. Promise: To recognize Jerusalem as the capital of Israel and oppose the creation of an independent Palestinian state.

Status: The President signed into law the "Jerusalem Bill" which recognizes Jerusalem as the capital of Israel. **✓ Promise Kept**

134. Promise: To modify foreign aid programs that promote democracy.

Status: The President signed into law the Assistance to New Independent States sponsored by Representative Richard Gephardt (D-Missouri). This is a bill for reform in emerging new democracies, and support and help for improved partnerships with Russia, Ukraine, and other new independent states of the former Soviet Union. **✓ Promise Kept**

135. Promise: To establish Radio Free Asia.

Status: No action taken.

SUMMARY:
Promises on International Relations Made—10
Action Taken On—9, or 90%
Achieved Substantial Results—9, or 90%

POVERTY AND WELFARE

136. Promise: To require welfare recipients who can work to find jobs or repay services with work in the community after two years of expanded assistance and training.

Status: The President signed the 1996 welfare reform bill that limits
✓ **Promise** lifetime eligibility to five years.
Kept

137. Promise: To create optional Individual Development Accounts for low-income Americans to encourage savings with federal matching funds.

Status: This idea was included in the Work and Responsibility Act pro-
✓ **Promise** posed in Congress and has recently been embraced by the
Kept GOP as part of a piece of tax legislation. Though it will not pass before the end of 1996, it will likely become law in the foreseeable future.

SUMMARY:
Promises on Poverty and Welfare Made —2
Action Taken On—2, or 100%
Achieved Substantial Results—2, or 100%

SOCIAL SECURITY

138. Promise: To raise earning limitations so recipients can collect more income along with their benefits.

Status: The President signed into law a provision that will gradually
✓ **Promise** increase the Social Security earnings limit to $30,000 by the
Kept year 2002. For 1996, the earnings limit is $11,520.

139. Promise: To consider higher taxes on benefits for wealthier recipients.

Status: This provision was included in budget FY94.

140. Promise: To ensure the Social Security System's solvency.

Status: Social Security Advisory Council undertakes periodic review surrounding the solvency of the Social Security System. Throughout his administration, President Clinton has steadfastly maintained that safeguarding the Social Security System and its benefits to recipients is a nonnegotiable item in budget negotiations.

SUMMARY:
Promises on Social Security Made—3
Action Taken On—3, or 100%
Achieved Substantial Results—3, or 100%

SPACE

141. Promise: To launch more ventures with Europe, Japan, and Russia.

Status: Funding was approved by Congress for the international space station.

142. Promise: To maintain NASA's fleet of space shuttles.

Status: NASA has reduced the operational costs of the shuttle fleet while continuing a safe flight program. Funding for the Space Station Freedom project continues.

143. Promise: To develop new, less costly launch systems.

On December 9, 1993, the nation watched as the Hubble Space Telescope (left) got back on schedule after a week and a half of problems with the vehicle's cargo bay. The space shuttle Endeavor lands at Edwards Air Force Base in California (below) after an 11-day mission in October of 1994.

Status: Presidential Directive (NSTC-PDD4) established a new launch policy to develop systems to lower costs.

✓ Promise Kept

144. Promise: To increase environmental research through NASA's "Mission to Planet Earth."

Status: Funding for this program has increased approximately 30 percent since January 1993.

✓ Promise Kept

145. Promise: To continue to use unmanned probes and robots to explore other planets.

Status: Under President Clinton, NASA has developed a space robot, "Ranger," that can refuel and repair satellites. It costs about $100 million dollars to build and launch a satellite, but it is useless if it breaks or runs out of fuel. Ranger can be launched from the shuttle or from a rocket and fly around for a month fixing and fueling dying satellites. This type of technology can produce consider- ✓ **Promise Kept** able savings.

The President honors the Apollo 11 astronauts at the White House.

146. Promise: To back away from President Bush's plans for exploration of the moon and Mars by U.S. astronauts, but continue scientific studies for internationally financed missions.

Status: Much of the savings will be achieved by sending robots in place

✓Promise of astronauts.
 Kept

> SUMMARY:
> Promises on Space Made—6
> Action Taken On—6, or 100%
> Achieved Substantial Results—6, or 100%

TAXES (Personal)

147. Promise: To raise tax rates on joint filers whose adjusted gross incomes are more than $200,000 or individuals whose AGIs are more than $150,000.

Status: Income tax rates were raised on the top 1.2 percent of tax-

✓Promise payers. Joint filers making over $180,000 in adjusted gross
 Kept income saw their income taxes increase. H&R Block, the
Wall Street Journal, and the Congressional Budget Office confirm that only the top 1.2 percent saw their income tax rates increase.

148. Promise: To increase the alternative minimum tax rate from 24 to 26 percent or 27 percent.

Status: Increased the alternative minimum tax rate from 24 to 26 per-

✓Promise cent and to 28 percent for high-income individuals.
 Kept

149. Promise: To require millionaires to pay a 10 percent surtax.

Status: An additional 10 percent surcharge was imposed on taxpayers with taxable income in excess of $250,000. **Promise Kept**

150. Promise: To offer middle-class families $60 billion in tax cuts over four years in the form of a $300 tax cut per couple or a $300-per-child tax credit.

Status: The President, in his Middle Class Ballot of Rights, has proposed a $60 billion tax cut over four years for middle-class families, including a $500-per-child tax credit. **Promise Kept**

151. Promise: To increase the Earned Income Tax Credit for the working poor.

Status: President Clinton included in his Economic Plan a historic expansion of the Earned Income Tax Credit (EITC) by $21 billion over five years to reward work over welfare. More than fifteen million households with incomes of $27,000 or less will be provided with either a new or increased EITC when the program is fully implemented. **Promise Kept**

> **SUMMARY:**
> **Promises on Personal Taxes Made—5**
> **Action Taken On—5, or 100%**
> **Achieved Substantial Results—5, or 100%**

TRADE

152. Promise: To continue international talks to renew the General Agreement on Tariffs and Trade while strengthening U.S. "Super 301" laws to punish nations with unfair trading practices unilaterally.

Status: The President signed the Uruguay Round Agreement Act into ✓Promise Kept law, creating the World Trade Organization on December 8, 1994. President Clinton reinstituted Super 301 through an Executive Order and has used it to bring trading partners to the table. He also extended Super 301 in GATT legislation.

153. Promise: To support the North American Free Trade Agreement as long as other accords can be reached on the environment and labor standards.

Status: NAFTA was signed into law on December 8, 1993. On January ✓Promise Kept 1, 1994, the U.S. opened a National Administrative Office to handle NAFTA-related labor issues. U.S exports to Mexico were 11 percent higher in 1995 than they were in 1993, the year before NAFTA was signed.

154. Promise: To ban U.S. trade negotiators and all senior Administration officials from working as lobbyists for foreign governments or businesses.

Status: Executive Order 12834 was signed on January 20, 1993, pro- ✓Promise Kept hibiting all senior appointees from working as lobbyists for foreign governments or businesses within five years of their employment termination.

SUMMARY:
   Promises on Trade Made—3
   Action Taken On—3, or 100%
   Achieved Substantial Results—3, or 100%

VETERANS

155. Promise: To oppose opening VA hospitals to nonveterans.

Status: VA hospitals remain closed to nonveterans.

156. Promise: To decrease waiting periods for outpatient care.

Status: To reduce waiting times, the Veterans Administration is developing telephone systems to make it easier for patients to make appointments so that outpatient care can be scheduled. To increase capacity, President Clinton's 1995 budget included funds for more outpatient facilities and VA is converting some underused inpatient facilities to outpatient care.

157. Promise: To notify disabled veterans of benefit changes in advance.

Status: Veterans whose benefit payments are to change are now notified at least 30 days in advance.

SUMMARY:
   Promises on Veterans Made—3
   Action Taken On—3, or 100%
   Achieved Substantial Results—3, or 100%

SCORE

As a candidate, the President advanced 157 separate campaign promises on his way to the Oval Office as tallied by the *Washington Post.* To date, the Clinton White House has taken action on 150.5 of those promises, or 96%. Of the 157 promises, he achieved substantial results on 136.5 of them, or 87%.

PART THREE

EXTRA CREDIT

In addition to the routine duties of a President, there is a certain "added value" that Americans have come to expect: leadership and vision. These intangibles could also be considered "extra credit." Modern-day Presidents are expected to perform miracles: make things right when they are wrong, show resolve in the face of adversity, deftly respond in times of crisis, inspire when all appears lost, and face down our foes without batting an eye. The ideal Chief Executive must also have compassionate qualities such as commitment, loyalty, the fortitude to look after those less fortunate, and the willingness to take on unpopular causes for the long-term good of the nation.

Leadership

Virtually every President, at one time or another during his term in office, has been tested by circumstances that exceed the norm. It is during these times that the country has often cried out for leadership in order that we as a nation could recover, heal our wounds, and, sometimes, mourn. During President Clinton's first term in office, he too has been confronted by a number of challenges that go beyond the pale of everyday leadership.

The North Korean Nuclear Threat

For several years the North Korean nuclear crisis has festered under a veil of diplomatic accords and nonbinding agreements. For a time, the Democratic Republic of North Korea, under the leadership of communist strongman Kim Il Sung, gave the West and the International Atomic Energy Agency every reason to believe that their government was committed to compliance, signing the Nuclear Non-Proliferation Treaty in 1985, and agreeing to a nonnuclear agreement with South Korea in 1991. What's more, when Pyongyang announced the next month that it would allow inspections of its nuclear program (formally agreed to in 1985), the Bush Administration, perceiving good will, agreed to cancel planned military exercises with South Korea. This intelligence was passed on to the Clinton Administration when the President took office in 1993, although the debate as to the seriousness of the North Korean nuclear program continued to rage on at the State Department.

Then in March of that year, only two months into his first term, President Clinton faced his first foreign policy crisis when the North Koreans abruptly barred International Atomic Energy Agency officials from inspecting a suspected reprocessing site at Youngbyon. To make matters worse, Kim Il Sung, without warning, announced that his regime

would abandon the 1985 Non-Proliferation Treaty, triggering a nuclear standoff. The gravity of the situation was underscored when CIA and Pentagon analysts reported that the North Korean nuclear program was surging ahead, that construction of the country's second nuclear reactor, a 200-megawatt facility capable of producing 55 to 60 kilos of plutonium annually, was well under way. Intelligence sources also reported that the designs of both North Korean reactors were geared toward bombmaking rather than the production of electricity. Even more compelling was the fact that the second reactor, capable of producing enough plutonium for roughly 10 weapons a year, was scheduled to become fully operational by 1996.

President Clinton and his national security advisors took this threat quite seriously, recognizing that the North Korean nuclear program, if left unabated, was only a short time away from developing nuclear missiles that could hit China, Russia, and Japan. Moreover, it was no secret that nations such as Iran, Iraq, and Syria have been actively in the market for missile technology. Accordingly, following a strategy that had as its linchpin the goal of convincing North Korea that it would be better served by forsaking its nuclear program and seeking economic integration into the world community, the Clinton Administration pursued every conceivable diplomatic channel to resolve the crisis.

For the next 16 months, the United States enlisted the support of the United Nations Security Council and third-party intermediaries, even participating in two rounds of unprecedented official face-to-face negotiations in Geneva, aimed at developing ties between the two countries.

By May 1994, while some progress was made—North Korea was voluntarily complying with the spirit of the 1985 Treaty—the Clinton Administration decided that stronger measures were necessary to end the crisis. First, head State Department negotiator Robert Galluci announced U.S. plans to offer a fresh initiative to the North Korean government, which would include high-level talks long sought by Pyongyang. Galluci, having just returned from Asia and consultations with the Chinese, South Korean, and Japanese governments about the stalemate, was well aware that he'd shored up the necessary support to back up the initiative. Then, several days later, Defense Secretary William J. Perry delivered a major foreign policy address in which he spelled out in the gravest of terms the ramifications of failure by the United States to stop the North Korean nuclear weapons program. Secretary Perry listed war in South Korea, the spread of nuclear weapons to other hostile countries, and a nuclear arms race that would drag in the Japanese. Further, he warned that the United States is committed to defending South Korea if war breaks out and pledged that the combined forces of the two nations would decisively and rapidly defeat any attack from the North. In short, the Pentagon head issued the North Koreans a choice; continue the program and face the consequences, possibly including war, or drop it and accept economic aid and normal relations with the United States and its allies.

This "line in the sand" approach was only one component of a complex White House strategy to stop the nuclear threat. The next, and most controversial, step came in June when the Clinton Administration announced that it would pursue economic sanctions against North Korea if some progress was not made soon. Imposing economic sanctions, while sometimes effective, is the type of tactical move that generally has few supporters. Previous administrations had given us two enormous diplomatic failures with Jimmy Carter's ill-fated grain embargo and Ronald Reagan's gas pipeline sanctions, both against the U.S.S.R. In each case, America's European allies were inconvenienced far more than the Soviet Union. In the North Korean conflict, sanctions were supported by such an unlikely pairing as Rep. Newt Gingrich and Senator Bill Bradley.

Then on June 23, 1994, a break came as the United States, South Korea, and Japan appeared to reach agreement on political and economic sanctions against North Korea. In response, North Korean leader Kim Il Sung sent for the first time a conciliatory message, offering to "suspend" plutonium processing in exchange for U.S. diplomatic recognition and support.

Finally in late June an accord was reached. Through the crisis, President Clinton had established three non-negotiable conditions that

any agreement must have to be acceptable to the United States. First, the North Koreans must not reprocess spent plutonium removed recently from an experimental reactor. Second, they must not refuel the reactor, and third, they must permit international inspectors to maintain safeguards against nuclear proliferation. In reaching the accord, each of these conditions was met.

The Oklahoma City Bombing

Word of the decade's most unconscionable act of terrorism first came to the President in a whisper while he was in a meeting with Turkish Prime Minister Tansu Ciller. In a soft voice, White House Press Secretary Mike McCurry informed the President that there had been a bombing at a federal building in Oklahoma City. Minutes later, after the visiting Prime Minister was escorted to the Cabinet Room, White House Chief of Staff Leon Panetta gave the President the grisly details: about an hour earlier on the morning of April 19th, a huge explosion had destroyed half the Alfred P. Murrah building, certainly killing at least a hundred people. But there was more. A day care center, filled to capacity, was located on the first floor of the Murrah building, in the epicenter of the blast. The final death toll of the bombing was 169, including 19 children under the age of five.

Within hours President Clinton delivered his first official statement on the bombing. Speaking with a mixture of anger and empathy he labeled the bombers "evil cowards" and promised that they would be hunted down and "treated like killers." Then he assured the nation that as the investigation went forward, "we will be about our work."

Meanwhile, the Murrah building had been reduced to near rubble by the 4,800-pound bomb comprised of ammonium nitrate and fuel oil. Day- and night-rescue workers labored around the clock, their every move recorded by the cameras from every major network as well as those from other countries. They were supplemented by Red Cross workers, medical personnel, stretcher bearers, blood donors, and counselors at local relief shelters. At a memorial service for the victims on April 23, the Reverend Billy Graham asked, "Why does God allow...such a terrible thing to happen?" Lost for an answer, the Reverend said, "There's something about evil we will never understand."

The next Saturday the President, with the First Lady present, delivered the weekly radio address with 26 children assembled in the Oval Office to talk about the tragedy. On Sunday, President Clinton flew to Oklahoma to officiate at the first of many memorial services he would attend on behalf of the victims of the bombing.

On January 23, 1996, during his fourth State of the Union address, the President sought to share with the country some inspiration from that tragic event. "His name is Richard Dean. He is a 49-year-old Vietnam veteran who's worked for the Social Security Administration for 22 years now. Last year he was hard at work in the federal building in Oklahoma City when the blast killed 169 people and brought the rubble down all around him. He reentered that building four times. He saved the lives of three women. He's here with us this evening, and I want to recognize Richard and applaud both his public service and his extraordinary personal heroism."

The 1995 Budget Battle

Contentious and protracted budget fights between the Democrats and Republicans are nothing new. Among the more memorable were the 1982 battle pitting House Speaker Tip O'Neill head to head against President Ronald Reagan, and the 1989 economic package of George Bush in which he reneged on his promise not to raise taxes. So, it was no surprise in the fall of 1995, with no budget deal on the table and the federal government scheduled to run out of money by Thanksgiving, that House Speaker Newt Gingrich and his conservative Republican majority in Congress tried to seize the moment and strong-arm a budget bill through both chambers, claiming that it would balance the budget in seven years and, at the same time, offer a substantial upper class tax cut.

A "closed" sign hangs in the door of Smithsonian's Air and Space Museum in Washington on November 14, 1995, a result of the federal government shutdown.

What was surprising, however, was how far each side was willing to go to achieve victory.

The first skirmish in the historic budget battle of '95 occurred in mid-November when draft versions of the House budget made it clear that the Congressional Republicans and the President were miles apart in their thinking. For example, one version had the House budget and the White House $170 billion apart in funding Medicare alone. With no hope of a deal in sight, and the first government shutdown since 1981 approaching, House Speaker Gingrich engaged in a risky strategy in which he offered to send the White House a stopgap continuing spending resolution to keep the government open. However, unlike continuing resolutions in the past, the Speaker's proposed funding measure had strings attached that were unacceptable to the White House.

When the Republican resolutions finally reached his desk, one a stopgap spending bill and another that would temporarily raise the federal debt ceiling, President Clinton's reaction was not what Speaker Gingrich had hoped for. Instead of retreating, the President summarily vetoed both spending measures in short order, citing that Republican riders on each bill would make "deep and unwise" cuts in Medicare.

On the second day of the shutdown, Speaker Gingrich, in a moment of frustration, commented to a reporter that he'd been personally offended by his treatment aboard Air Force One on return from the funeral of slain Israeli Prime Minister Yitzhak Rabin. Angered that the President would not discuss the budget with him and that he was asked to disembark via the rear stairwell, the Speaker went on record as saying, "This is petty. I'm going to say up front it's petty, but that's part of why you ended up with us sending down a tougher stopgap measure." President Clinton, for his part, followed the high road, saying, "If it would get the government open, I'd be glad to tell the Speaker I'm sorry."

As a result of the impasse, on November 21, 1995, the federal government ran out of money and shut down. The impact was swift and instantaneous. That day, the federal government sent home over 800,000 "non-essential" workers at the height of the holiday season. The shutdown immediately brought government agencies, museums, parks, and laboratories to a standstill. Other visible signs of the shutdown were the closing of the Washington Monument and Mount Rushmore. For many Americans, the impact was truly devastating, as applications for Social Security or disability benefits were no longer being accepted at agency field offices because there were no employees to process them.

Employees deemed "essential," including national security, safety, and communications personnel, were ordered to stay on the job during the shutdown. Meanwhile, Treasury Secretary Robert Rubin juggled the federal books and tapped two civil service retirement funds in order to avert an unprecedented default on U.S. government obligations. By the second week of the shutdown GOP leaders were reeling from the fact that, despite the enormous chaos and havoc caused by the shutdown, the President had drawn a line and wasn't moving.

Newsweek wrote that "the Republican budget is skewed against the poor. Welfare, food stamps, and subsidized housing are all curbed. The working poor get little tax relief, because a tax provision benefiting them (the earned-income tax credit) is being scaled back. Taken together, these policies might lower the incomes of about 42 percent of the poorest fifth of families, according to a new study by the Urban Institute. Perhaps 7 percent of the 27 million Americans on food stamps might ultimately become ineligible, as would a quarter of those on welfare."

Although one short-term measure was passed to reopen the government for several days, stage two of the budget battle came the first week of December when Congress sent the President its latest version of the Balanced Budget Act of 1995. The Act contained cuts in funding levels for Medicaid and environmental protection, as well as rather large upper income tax cuts that were unacceptable to the White House. President Clinton vetoed the GOP-backed proposal, saying, "I believe their budget will do harm to our country. This is a choice the American people have to make between two very different visions of change."

In taking this stand President Clinton permanently changed the parameters of the debate. By vetoing the Republican balanced budget bill, the President made protecting Medicaid his number one imperative, saying that "if the Republicans keep insisting that the federal government retreat from the Medicaid business, the Republicans could forget about a budget agreement." Medicaid, often thought of as health care for the poor, is actually many programs in one, providing basic health coverage for 24 million poor children and adults, but they account for just one quarter of the program's $156 billion annual tab. The big cost comes from providing long-term care for 10 million elderly and disabled Americans. All told, Medicaid covers 2 in 4 American children, pays for 1 in 3 births, and finances more than half the nursing home care in the country.

With the battle lines drawn more clearly than ever, concrete, yet often contentious negotiations continued throughout the month of December to resolve the crisis. As the poll numbers measuring the Republicans' performance in the budget battle continued to plummet, a thaw came on the first weekend in January as President Clinton, seeking to keep the process moving, offered to support a seven-year balanced budget plan sponsored by Senate Minority Leader Tom Daschle (D-South Dakota). The President's endorsement came as a result of a Republican challenge that if the President would come out in support of any plan with a seven-year timetable, then they would pass a continuing resolution without strings and reopen the government. But, in response to President Clinton's concession in embracing the Daschle plan, the Congressional Republicans reneged on their offer.

Despite this, an unexpected break came the following Tuesday, when Senate Majority Leader Bob Dole broke ranks and proposed a continuing resolution to reopen the government. Although his fellow Republicans were outraged, his colleagues in the leadership, especially Speaker Gingrich, slowly began to admit that they were playing a losing hand. The media were running stories nightly of the plights of furloughed workers and darkened embassies and closed Social Security offices. This change in thinking came after yet another no-holds-barred negotiating session was held at the White House in which only the senior negotiators were allowed to attend. By Friday morning, Speaker Gingrich addressed the Republican House members, briefly explaining a plan to return the 800,000 federal employees to work. Knowing that the public was not buying what *Time* magazine was calling the Republican "blackmail strategy," he announced plans to reverse course, acknowledging for the first time that it was "morally indefensible not to pay federal workers."

Later that day, on January 5, 1996, the House approved a plan to put all 800,000 federal workers back on the job through January 26th and give them back pay from December 25th when the latest shutdown began. And President Clinton, having taken a stand to safeguard Medicaid as well as other programs protecting the disadvantaged and working Americans, was able to claim more than just a temporary victory as the Republican controlled Congress passed an ongoing spending measure in April of 1996, effectively funding the government through the end of the fiscal year.

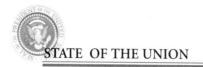

The Rabin Assassination

For Yitzhak Rabin, the celebration at Kings of Israel Square in Central Tel Aviv on November 4, 1995, was a moment to savor. A joyous throng of 100,000 people had gathered to celebrate peace with songs and speeches, and throughout the event, the Israeli Prime Minister seemed to be enjoying the upbeat mood of the crowd. With peace treaties in force with both the Palestinians and Jordan, he dismissed threats from right wing extremists comparing him to Hitler.

When 27-year-old Israeli law student Yigal Amir fired three shots at Rabin that evening, his intent was not just to murder the Prime Minister in cold blood, but to strike a fatal blow to the Middle Eastern peace process. Rabin, not unlike Abraham Lincoln, was a leader of a divided nation, gunned down by one of his own countrymen as he fought for peace.

President Clinton had recently made history with his friend, Rabin. Together the two heads of state had worked diligently for the preceding three years to build a peace between Israel and its surrounding neighbors. The joint efforts of the two men had yielded surprisingly positive results. Ongoing initiatives had resulted in great progress in granting Palestinians autonomy in return for security guarantees. In September of 1993 President Clinton hosted Rabin and PLO head Yasser Arafat at the White House for the signing of the Israeli-Palestinian peace accord. Not long after, a similar event was held to commemorate the first ever peace treaty between Israel and Jordan.

Despite this success, most analysts agree that the peace among Israel and its Arab neighbors is a fragile one. Israelis are equally divided on the issue of trading land for peace. While some would willingly accept a Palestinian state, religious settlers believe that God gave them the West Bank, and no political leader could summarily give it away with a treaty. So when President Clinton boarded Air Force One to lead the American delegation attending the funeral of the slain leader, he faced the challenge of not just paying tribute to his close friend and ally, but at the same time sending the right signal to the many disparate groups that would be represented. With Rabin's passing, there was a concern that the peace process could begin to backslide.

At the slain leader's funeral, President Clinton led a delegation constructed to demonstrate an unmistakable show of American support, both of Israel and the peace process. White House Press Secretary Mike McCurry said it was the President's view that the United States owes, as a "lasting memorial" to Yitzhak Rabin, "our best efforts to advance the peace process." Accordingly, the U.S. delegation was purposely composed of former Presidents Jimmy Carter and George Bush, former Secretary of State Cyrus Vance, over 40 members of the House and Senate, as well as 50 or more lawmakers, and community and religious leaders. President Clinton said the size and composition of the delegation was meant to send "the message that the United States still stands as a genuine friend and a partner to the people of Israel, Republicans and Democrats alike. We have decades of dedication to the cause of peace here.... The United States is standing with Israel and standing for the cause of peace." Israeli Ambassador to the United States Itamar Rabinovich characterized the American display as "awesome."

During his eulogy of Rabin—very personal in tone, filled with anecdotes depicting the depth and warmth of their friendship—the President could not help but show his grief, saying "The American people mourn with you and the loss of your leader, and I mourn with you, for he was my partner and friend. Every moment we shared was a joy, because he was a good man, and an inspiration because he was also a great man. Your Prime Minister was a martyr for peace, but was a victim of hate. Surely we must learn from his martyrdom that if people cannot let go of the hatred of their enemies, they risk sowing the seeds of hatred among themselves.

"I ask you, the people of Israel, on behalf of my nation that knows its long litany of loss from Abraham Lincoln to President Kennedy to Martin Luther King, don't let that happen to you."

After the service, the President held separate meetings with every Middle Eastern leader in attendance and used the opportunity to solidify unity and continuity in the peace process.

The Ron Brown Tragedy

On April 3, 1996, a military style 737 jetliner carrying Secretary of Commerce Ron Brown and 34 others crashed into a mountainside as it tried to land in Dubrovnik, near the Dalmation coast in Croatia. All aboard were killed. The purpose of the flight was a trade mission sponsored by the Commerce Department to develop a telecommunications infrastructure in war-torn Bosnia. Many on board were telecommunications executives and venture capitalists, part of Secretary Brown's team of specialists who would help rebuild the region.

The impact of the tragedy was quickly felt far and wide, in part because America had lost one of its most gifted and capable political figures, and because all of the people on board were of such talent and character. The President, who knew many of the victims personally and counted the Commerce Secretary as one of his closest friends, called for a national period of mourning. He greeted the loved ones of the victims at Dover Air Force Base in Delaware as the bodies of the dead arrived from Germany. There, while the flag-draped caskets were unloaded, the President consoled the families and friends and praised the government workers and business executives who risked their lives to give the people of Bosnia a chance to rebuild their country. "The 33 lives show us the best of America. They are a stern rebuke to the cynicism that is all too familiar today. For as family after family told the Vice President and Hillary and me today, their loved ones were proud of what they were doing. They believed in what they were doing. They believed in this country. They believed we could make a difference. And more important they were a glowing testimony to the power of an individual to improve their own lives and elevate the lives of others and make a better future for others. Nearly 5,000 miles from home they went out to help people build their own homes and roads, to turn on the lights in cities darkened by war, to restore the everyday interchange of people working and living together with something to look forward to and a dream to raise their own children by. They were all patriots. In their memory and in their honor, let us rededicate our lives to our country and to our fellow citizens. In their memory and in their honor, let us resolve to continue their mission of peace and healing and progress."

When President Clinton finished, he walked over and took a seat next to Secretary Brown's widow, Alma, whose husband he'd eulogized earlier in the week, and would honor many more times in the days to come as "one of the best advisers and ablest people I ever knew, and he was very, very good at everything he did. Whether he was Commerce Secretary or a civil rights leader or something else, he was always out there just giving it his all." Together the President and Mrs. Brown sat on the runway with the families and loved ones of the "33 patriots" while the memorial service continued, and the nation dealt with the loss of one of its favorite sons.

President Clinton escorts Alma Brown, widow of Commerce Secretary Ron Brown, after arriving at Dover Air Force Base on April 6, 1996.

Vision for the Future

The best place President Clinton's vision for the future can be found is in his own words. On January 23, 1996, during the final State of the Union address of the President's first term, he stated his vision of the seven major challenges facing the country, and his call to action on how to deal with them.

I. "Our first challenge is to cherish our children and strengthen America's families. Family is the foundation of American life. If we have stronger families, we will have a stronger America."

Call to Action:

• Congress should pass a bipartisan welfare reform bill that reinforces the basic American values—work, responsibility, and family.

• Congress should pass meaningful health insurance reform, allowing people to retain coverage when they change jobs, and preventing insurance companies from denying coverage due to pre-existing conditions.

• Families must work harder to stay together and avoid domestic violence at all costs.

• The media and the entertainment industry should take into account the needs of children when creating movies, CDs and television shows.

II. "People...need education and training.... More and more Americans are finding that the education of their childhood simply doesn't last a lifetime."

Call to Action:

• Make up to $10,000 of annual college tuition tax-deductible; expanding work-study to help one million young Americans through college by the year 2000; providing $1,000 merit scholarships for five percent of high school graduates; and increasing the number of Pell Grants for students in financial need.

• Every state, community and school should adopt national standards of excellence and give schools and teachers more flexibility for grassroots reform.

• Every state should give parents the right to choose the public school their children will attend and allow parents, teachers, and administrators to form new charter schools.

• All parents should become more involved in their children's education.

III. "People who work hard still need support to get ahead in the new economy."

Call to Action:

• Raise the minimum wage, providing working Americans the opportunity to lift themselves and their families out of poverty.

• Consolidate overlapping, antiquated federal job-training programs into a simple $2,600 job-training voucher that will allow unemployed workers the freedom to choose the best training programs.

• Enable Americans to save for their retirement by increasing pension portability, enhancing pension protection, and expanding coverage, while making it easier for small businesses to offer pension plans to their workers.

• Preserve and strengthen Medicare and Medicaid.

• Fight health care fraud and abuse.

IV. "We have begun to find a way to reduce crime, forming community partnerships with local police forces to catch criminals and prevent crime. This strategy, called community policing, is clearly working. Violent crime is coming down all across America. In New York City, murders are down 25%, in St. Louis 18%, in Seattle 32%. But we still have a long way to go before our streets are safe and our people are free from fear."

Call to Action:

- Congress should pass legislation providing tougher sentences for gun-wielding drug dealers and gang members.
- Submit to Congress legislation that gives prosecutors the discretion to prosecute juvenile offenders as adults.
- Call on states to ensure that prisoners serve at least 85 percent of their sentences, and to follow the federal lead in requiring that all of those arrested be drug tested as they enter the criminal justice system.

V. "Because of a generation of bipartisan effort we do have cleaner water and air, lead levels in children's blood have been cut by 70 percent and toxic emissions from factories have been cut in half.... But we still have much to do."

Call to Action:

- Congress should move to abandon proposals that force taxpayers to pick up the tab for environmental cleanup.
- Congress should move to re-examine and reverse those policies that endanger or weaken health and safety programs.
- American businesses should take greater initiative in protecting the environment.
- Replace one-size-fits-all regulations with results-focused programs.
- Continue to work with state and community leaders and businesses to find better ways to protect our natural resources and provide economic opportunities for all Americans.

VI. "Because of American leadership, more people than ever before live free and at peace.... All over the world, even after the Cold War, people still look to us and trust us to help them seek the blessings of peace and freedom.... Where our interests and our values are at stake, and where we can make a difference, America must lead. We must not be isolationist."

Call to Action:

• Intensify the fight against terrorism and organized crime at home and abroad by working for tougher enforcement and more cross-border cooperation.

• Secure a truly comprehensive nuclear test ban treaty.

• Outlaw poison gas forever by ratifying the Chemical Weapons Convention.

• Aggressively combat international drug-trafficking by working closely with other countries, providing military support and initiating anti-corruption efforts to stem the flow of drugs.

• Admit the first new NATO members since the end of the Cold War and maintain a partnership with Russia.

VII. "Our seventh challenge is really America's challenge to those of us in this hallowed hall tonight: to reinvent our government and make our democracy work."

Call to Action:

• Pass the first truly bipartisan campaign finance reform bill in a generation that will limit campaign spending and open the airwaves to all candidates.

• Forge new relationships with communities by creating performance partnerships. Together, the federal, state, and local governments will set goals and the communities will decide how best to meet them.

• Establish single points of contact for communities with more than 150,000 residents. The single point of contact will hopefully resolve problems these communities may have with agencies of the federal government.

Photo Credits

© **AP/Wide World:** Pages 20, 30, 32, 33, 36, 40, 42, 47, 52, 63 (bottom), 68, 71, 73, 75, 77, 82, 87, 91, 92, 102 (left), 105, 131, 148, 164, 171.

© **Phil Matt:** Page 72.

© **UNIPHOTO:** Back Cover, Pages 6, 15, 25, 49, 54, 59, 60, 61, 63 (top), 64, 86, 88, 98, 102 (right), 149.